LIFE IN THE FISH BOWL

Building Up Church Workers

Tom Rogers

CPH

SAINT LOUIS

Copyright © 1996 Concordia Publishing House
3558 S. Jefferson Avenue, St. Louis, MO 63118-3968
Manufactured in the United States of America.

Library of Congress Cataloging-in-Publication Data

Rogers, Tom, 1952–
    Life in the fishbowl: building up church workers/ Tom Rogers.
      p.   cm.
    ISBN 0-570-04871-0
    1. Church work—Lutheran Church—Missouri Synod. 2. Lutheran Church—Missouri Synod—Membership. 3. Lutheran Church—United States—Membership.   I. Title
    BV4403.R64   1996
    248.8'9—dc20   96-14458

1 2 3 4 5 6 7 8 9 10   05 04 03 02 01 00 99 98 97 96

In memory of Claude James Christopher—
mechanic, philosopher, fishing buddy, Grandfather—
whose devotion to his Lord continues
to build up this church worker.

CONTENTS

AMEN!

A wonderful quartet assists our congregation in worship. Each Sunday's quartet is made up of any four of about 16 people who practice for, and participate in, this ministry. The idea is that we'd like to share the wealth and the responsibility with as many members as possible.

Recently a brand-new member joined the group and participated in worship for the first time. After the service, I had a cup of coffee with the quartet and thanked them for their tremendous service. Three of the four said thank you. The fourth person, the new person, said, "Really? Did we really do all right?" I said, "Yes, indeed!" and the conversation continued in another vein.

After a couple minutes, in the midst of a discussion about the baseball season, our newest singer said, "Well, I hope we did all right this morning. I'm not so sure." I briefly reassured him that the quartet did a magnificent job, just as they always do, and went back to discussing baseball. A few minutes later, as we were discussing the amount of the California State Lottery (can you discuss lotteries on church property?), the new vocalist said, "I sure hope the congregation was blessed by our singing." The light finally began to flicker in my dull brain. This poor soul was insecure; he required approval, affirmation, and support. As I gave it to him one more time, and this time added a pat on the back to my accolades, I thought how tough it must be to go through life so insecure.

As a rule, God doesn't seem to let me get away with those kinds of thoughts. At lunch that afternoon, one of my daughters said, "Daddy, that was a pretty good sermon today." My mind immediately began to race. What does she mean "pretty good sermon," and why does she say "today"? Aren't all my sermons good? So I asked her, "What do you mean by that? Are my sermons not good sometimes?" She gave me the smug smile of a 13-year-old, put her arms around my shoulders, and said, "Dad, don't worry about it. The people keep paying you, don't they?" That comment provided little solace.

I asked my wife if she thought that the quality of my work had begun to suffer. She replied with "not this again." She went on to remind me that at the beginning of my ministry, I used to force her to listen to my sermons before I preached them. Then I asked her what she thought of them. If she made some negative comment or registered some critical opinion, I was demoralized. After a few months, I realized that I was placing her in a horrible position and decided to face my preaching opportunities like a "big boy."

I share this story and this confession with you because I believe that all of us who work for the Lord, both professionally and on a volunteer basis, have a powerful need for approval. We all are familiar with the uncomfortable feeling of doubt as we scan the faces of those we have just preached to, sung to, or taught. We hope and pray that someone will acknowledge that our work is good.

If there were ever any doubt that human beings lost their sense of security at the fall in the Garden of Eden, church workers remove it. Each of us knows that we are naked before the Lord and the people we serve, and we seek to cover ourselves with the fig leaves of hard work; years of experience; someone else's apparently successful style; or the time-honored excuse that we work so hard, we're tired and unprepared. Like the original fig leaves, these cover-ups wither and fade. We wind up naked once again, scratching uncontrollably in some very embarrassing places.

But God has a solution for us: Instead of the fig leaves of excuses, we are invited, even enjoined, to "put on the full armor of God so that you can take your stand against the devil's schemes." Satan is at his wiliest when he is trying to silence the voices and confidence of the servants of Christ. And the best way to do that is to get us to question whether or not we have the authority and the ability to share Jesus with the church and world.

The people of God often need some encouragement in their lives. Some begin to believe their lives are so filled with sin, trouble, and disappointment that God can't possibly love them, much less use them. Yet the Scriptures provide numerous examples of people whom God uses even though they are less than perfect. Let me explain.

Christian mothers often confess that they feel completely unable to manage their families' schedules. They forget to pick up children from athletic practices because they have been busy taking other children to medical appointments. And their husbands—who believe they are liberated men and say they're ready to pitch in and fix meals and bathe children and help with homework—often revolt and add to the chaos. "I'm so unorganized," these moms say. Perhaps they are, but where would we be as the church of Jesus Christ if it hadn't been for 4,999 people who were so anxious to hear Jesus preach one day that they forgot their lunches? Those forgetful, unorganized souls enabled the Lord Jesus to show His glory in a wonderful way by feeding 5,000 ordinary folks like you and me. Our inability to be perfect does one glorious thing: It demonstrates to the world the power of God.

And where would we be without the thief on the cross? He would never be declared a candidate certified for ministry within the church. He would never have been asked to teach a Sunday school class. Although he would have most assuredly been invited, I'm sure he would never have attended a men's Bible study. But at the hands of the Almighty, he has become the comfort and joy of the "lost causes," those who believe that their lives have been so deplorable that God could never love them. This unnamed man has been a source of comfort and strength for millions of people over the centuries.

At that specific moment, I'm sure neither the 4,999 who needed lunch nor the thief on the cross fancied themselves servants of the Most High God. But in retrospect, I'm sure they would celebrate the fact that they were. I believe that all of us imperfect servants of the Lord Jesus can celebrate too. God's power is great enough to use even our mistakes for His glory.

And as God anticipated the mistakes, He also provided the solution for our mistakes in His Son, Jesus. I love the way the apostle Paul, under the guidance of the Holy Spirit, addressed the church at Corinth. You might recall that this church was filled with trouble and troubled people. Their celebration of Holy Communion was a danger to their spiritual and physical health. They were hopelessly divided into camps and parties, and their sexual misconduct could rival that of Hollywood! (I can say that because I live in Southern California.) But Paul wrote:

> I always thank God for you because of His grace given you in Christ Jesus. For in Him you have been enriched in every way—in all your speaking and in all your knowledge—because our testimony about Christ was confirmed in you. Therefore you do not lack any spiritual gift as you eagerly wait for our Lord Jesus Christ to be revealed. *(1 Corinthians 1:4–7)*

The people in Corinth were never perfect, but they were effective. It is the same with you and me. We have never been, nor will we ever be, perfect, but through the power of the Holy Spirit, we will always be effective. Let me repeat that: You will always be effective, even if that effectiveness doesn't seem apparent to you. The Word of the Lord is clear, "My word that goes out from

My mouth: It will not return to Me empty, but will accomplish what I desire and achieve the purpose for which I sent it" (Isaiah 55:11). What better affirmation could we look for? God assures us we cannot fail because He's in charge.

In a world where people get voted into a hall of fame because they got on base one out of every three times (which means they failed miserably two out of every three times) and I can be elected a public servant because I might be the lesser of two evils rather than because I'm the best person in the race, God comes to us and says, "You can't miss. You will always help Me."

Therefore, when we walk away from sermons, songs, lessons, visits, Sunday school lessons, and counseling sessions, we get to hear the comforting words of God, "Well done, good and faithful servant!" These words, for Jesus' sake, are spoken from God to us whenever we serve in His name. They lift us up in the face of a world that seems bent on bringing us down. So if that's God's Word to us, then that also should be our word to one another in church professions.

As a brother speaking with his brothers and sisters, let me say this. If you have listened to a brother's words or if you have observed a sister's service to the Lord, don't walk away from that experience without doing one of the following things. Affirm the efforts of your brother and sister, congratulate the person, tell him or her that you appreciate the communication of the Word of God. Shame on you if you don't affirm them.

That is why the early church chose to retain the exclamation "Amen!" from its Old Testament roots. It's a word of affirmation. When the people of God speak it after a presentation, they let the presenter know that he or she faithfully has spoken the Word of God and is a valued member of the fellowship. How many times have we walked away from a presentation to *our colleagues* in a cloud of silence so thick it could close an airport? What has happened over the centuries? Have we forgotten how to pronounce *Amen?* No, I'm afraid the truth is that we have forgotten how to *feel* Amen. We are so critical of one another that we find faults with anyone, even our dearest and closest friends. We have become like starving people penned up in the same room with one package of Twinkies snack cakes. You know that the chance of getting even a bite is astronomical, but if you can't have any, then you're going to make sure no one else can either. Those who are deprived of affirmation generally deprive others of affirmation.

But we are not deprived of affirmation. We all have received affirmation aplenty in our baptisms. That was and is God's "Amen!" to us. Let's make the phrases "Thank you!" "Nice job!" and "I'm proud of you!" permeate our working relationships. They make a tremendous difference.

When I help couples prepare for marriage, the first thing we work on is their ability to affirm each other. I ask them to look at each other and answer this question: "Why is it, that in a world filled with thousands of people you probably could have spent the rest of your lives with, you have chosen this person?" The words that follow always amaze me. Couples say words that build each other up. They discover that affirmation is a wonderful thing to do for each other. This exercise helps them look forward to blessing each other all their lives.

God has affirmed us, and now He invites us to affirm one another. May we do such a good job of affirming one another that no member of our circles has to fish for a compliment ever again. Amen? Amen!

PRAYER

Dear Lord, thank You for affirming us through Your Son, Jesus Christ. Enable us to speak the *Amen* of affirmation to one another and to your people whom we serve in Jesus' name. In His name we pray. Amen.

2

BLESSED ARE THE CRITICS

I've been doing it so long it doesn't seem strange to me anymore, but it sure seemed strange to my secretary. As I open my mail, whether it's a form letter or a short handwritten note, I always check the signature before I begin reading. "Looking for a bomb?" she asked. "Exactly," I replied. She looked confused. I tried to explain.

My first year of ministry was a real challenge. My biggest liability was that I was new. That meant everything I did—from preaching to parking my car—was different. I worked hard to smother the people with love and care. Most folks responded well, but some just couldn't get over the fact that I was new and things were different.

One of those folks took it upon himself to write me a letter and share his unhappiness. The envelope was addressed to "Mr. Rogers" not "Rev. Rogers," and the letter's greeting read, "Tom." The author proceeded to tell me I was a poor excuse for a minister. He said I had no sense of sacredness or tradition. He went on to say I was still a young man and so still had time to retrain myself for a more suitable vocation. He signed his epistle, "A concerned soul."

That was it. No name. No offended brother or sister to whom I could go and seek reconciliation. I was hurt, insulted, angry. As I contemplated what I considered a cowardly act, I asked myself again and again who could have done such a cruel deed. The devil had a heyday with my mind. Every one of the dear people in that wonderful congregation became a potential suspect. When speaking the glorious words of absolution, I wanted to say, "In the stead and by the command of my Lord Jesus Christ I forgive you all of your sins, except for the crummy pagan who wrote me the unsigned letter." When folks knelt at the altar, I wanted to hold the precious body of Christ at eye level and ask, "Did you write the letter?" Upon hearing "No," I would say, "Okay then, the body of Christ is given for you." I began to seriously doubt my skill. My self-confidence was as low as the devil's sense of fair play. I honestly thought about resigning and leaving in shame and anger.

Then I ran into a magnificent passage in Scripture—2 Corinthians 5:16: "From now on we regard no one from a worldly point of view. Though we once regarded Christ in this way, we do so no longer."

We once regarded Christ from a worldly point of view. Does that mean Jesus got criticized? Could it mean that someone was bold enough to suggest that the Sermon on the Mount was too long or boring? Could people have left worship opportunities that Jesus led, such as Passover, and said, "I didn't get anything out of it"? Do you think anyone criticized the way He dressed or the stance He took on poor people or the government? Don't you wonder if people followed Him around just to count the congregation and then were only too happy to announce that He didn't attract as many as last year? Is it out of the realm of possibility to think that someone told Jesus that He should have remained a carpenter or should think about moving to another congregation? According to the Scriptures, that's exactly what happened. Jesus got His own share of unsigned critical letters. And as the Scriptures also say, "A servant is not above his master." Suddenly I didn't feel so bad about the letter. In fact, in a strange way, I was proud of it. It demonstrated that, if nothing else, my ministry wasn't going unnoticed.

I'd love to tell you that criticism doesn't bother me anymore. I'd love to tell you that, but I can't. Criticism still bothers me, but it doesn't destroy me because of Paul's words: "From now on we regard no one from a worldly point of view." Paul is saying the letters don't count. We are the servants of Christ, called by His grace. He has chosen us for His service. We may fumble, fall, fail, and fade, but God still claims us as His own and makes us His servants. Therefore, we can't let the criticizers get us down. It would only make it look as though Jesus doesn't have the power to use imperfect people like us nowadays, like He did in the good ol' days of Peter, James, John, and Saul of Tarsus. We get to go about our ministries day in and day out, accepting our mistakes and watching God use them for the good of His kingdom.

A dear friend of mine learned this lesson early in his ministry. Shortly after he arrived at his first church, one of the women of the congregation told him that her 20-year-old unmarried daughter was about to give birth and insisted on bringing the baby into her mother's modest home. This woman, in her mid-50s, was divorced and supporting herself and her three young children. Money and space were tight. If worry about finances and room weren't enough, the soon-to-be grandmother knew that her daughter had a history of instability—here one day, gone the next. The grandmother-to-be insisted that her daughter give this baby up for adoption. Because her daughter kept refusing, the woman called in her secret weapon—my friend. As a young pastor, he undoubtedly would be able to convince this young woman that adoption was the only sensible and, for that matter, Christian thing to do.

His orders were clear. The whole congregation was praying for him and cheering him on. He went to see the young woman and talked and talked and talked to no avail. Her mind was made up, and no pastor, young or old, was going to change it. She was keeping her baby and that was that.

The message that went through the congregation was not flattering. "Pastor talked to her, but he couldn't do any good." It was unanimous. He had failed. The baby was born, and he was big and healthy. He was baptized and taken to his grandmother's home. Everyone's worst fears were realized. It was a tough, tough time for that family.

Sometime during the third year of that little boy's life, my friend's brother came to stay with him for an extended vacation. During his visit, he met this young mother, fell in love with her and her son, and got married. Now 15 years later, the child is the pride and joy of the family. My friend may have failed in the eyes of the congregation, but God didn't fail. He worked through human weakness to achieve His purpose. Once again grace triumphed.

That's why I don't read unsigned letters or let criticism tear me apart. I've learned that I don't have the last word on the success or failure of my ministry—God does. He has the last word about the success of your ministry as well. Therefore, we can approach criticism and criticizers from a Christ-centered perspective. Just as Jesus loved His detractors, we can love ours. They, too, are baptized children of God. God can speak through them as well as us. When they approach us as the Scriptures direct, face to face, then we should listen carefully, react respectfully, and implement those changes and ideas that are good. And we should thank our critics for their help. Only people who want Jesus to increase and themselves to decrease are capable of doing that. That's the kind of people God has made us. For us, criticism is a chance to cling to Christ and His power for strength in our lives.

When I arrived at the church I'm presently serving, I discovered that 15 ordained clergymen were members of the congregation. When I shared that fact with friends and colleagues, most told me I'd be crazy to step into a situation like that. They all cringed when I accepted the position. "Every Sunday will be a report card day for you," said a close friend.

Much to my delight, my ministry at Abiding Savior has been an incredible blessing, and the 15 clergymen have been a real source of encouragement and help. The other day, one of those clergymen asked me why I had thought I could handle the potential criticism they could have brought. I thought for a moment and said, "A guy wrote me a letter once, and it changed my life." My only regret is that I'll never be able to thank him.

PRAYER

Jesus, You withstood the attacks of Your detractors with courage and with grace. Remind us daily that our worth is in You, not in us. Help us deal with our critics with the same courage and grace. In Your name we pray. Amen.

3

FAMILY AND PERSONAL TIME

Our first child was born by Caesarean section. That caught both my wife and me by surprise. Despite the surprise, everything worked out fine, and God delivered into our arms a beautiful little girl. When we discovered that we were expecting again, the obstetrician examined my wife and told us when the due date would be. He went on to mention that we really could pick another date near that time because this baby also would need to be delivered by Caesarean section. "Once you've had one baby by Caesarian section," he said, "you should have all your babies by Caesarean section."

That sounded great to me, but my wife protested. She boldly announced to the doctor that she was going to have this baby naturally. The doctor, a fine Southern gentleman, said, "Well then, ma'am, let me tell you about the mortality rates for mothers and babies when a Caesarean birth is followed by a natural birth." He painted a rather bleak picture of this pattern, doing everything he could to discourage her from trying such a thing.

I believed him. My wife disagreed. She was convinced that this baby should enter the world naturally. I hoped and prayed that sometime during the next six or seven months she would somehow come to her senses. She didn't.

It didn't seem like such a bad thing until I realized that I was supposed to take our youth group to Disney World about three weeks before the baby was to be born. "Should I go or shouldn't I?" I asked the doctor. He said to go ahead and enjoy the trip.

I went. Things were going fine. After a great day at the Magic Kingdom, I was planning to take the kids out to dinner. We made a quick stop at our motel to get cleaned up before dinner. When I arrived at my room, a note was attached to the door: "Call Baptist Hospital. Your wife is having a baby." I did, and she was.

I made quick arrangements to fly from Orlando to New Orleans. Unfortunately, I had to fly from Orlando to Atlanta and from Atlanta to New Orleans. When I called the hospital, I learned that my wife would probably deliver the baby before my plane landed. As my plane left Orlando, I knew something would happen before I got to Atlanta. I asked God to make that "something" the birth of my healthy daughter, but the only thing that ran through my head was the obstetrician's words, "Let me tell you about the mortality rates for mothers and babies when a Caesarean birth is followed by a natural birth." I could only look into the darkness 36,000 feet above the ground and pray. When I landed in

Atlanta, I ran to a telephone and learned my wife was fine, as was my daughter.

I had begun to learn an important lesson about personal and family time, the significance of which I didn't fully understand until about 1992. That's when my 10-year-old daughter began to comprehend why her father wasn't there for her birth. "I just wasn't as important to you as the youth group, was I, Dad?" I can tell her, "No, honey, you've always been the most important thing in Daddy's life" until I'm blue in the face. But chances are she won't believe it unless she sees this confession lived out day after day.

And that isn't easy. Ministry is a people business, and people's needs don't always fit easily into an eight-to-five work schedule. Just like doctors and lawyers, we ministers have all been stopped in supermarkets and restaurants by people who would like to share a problem or a concern. And because people are human, they have a tendency to put their needs above yours. I always chuckle when I make my way to the rest room at church and folks stop me to ask a question. My hand is on the door and I hear, "Pastor, do you have a minute?" I'm always tempted to answer, "I do now, but they tell me that when I get older, I won't." Don't people understand that I really need time to take care of personal business? They don't unless I tell them.

Part of our responsibility as church workers is to let the people we serve know what our personal and family needs are. I am convinced that how we care for our own families enables us to be a strong witness for Christ and a good example for those we serve. We hear colleagues described as good preachers or good teachers, excellent counselors, or capable administrators. We describe a member as a wonderful family man, an outstanding mother, a dedicated father, or a polite child. Isn't it strange that church workers are almost never characterized in those terms? That doesn't necessarily suggest that church workers are horrible family members. What it probably suggests is that we haven't done a good job of sharing with others that our families are the most important gifts God has given us besides our faith in Christ. The old bromide "Deeds speak louder than words" comes to mind. A fellow who misses his daughter's birth because he's on a youth trip shouldn't be surprised if church members expect him to be at their beck and call, even if the situation isn't urgent.

There are both positive and not-so-positive ways to get the word out about your need for private time. It may not be the wisest decision to call attention to your work schedule in your Sunday bulletin, your newsletter, or your monthly calendar. The most powerful communication tool you and I have is our own mouths. Who hasn't discovered that a word shared from the chancel during announcements is much more effective than a message in the church bulletin? Taking the time to tell people personally, "Friday is my day off, and I really try to keep it free for myself and my family," shows your congregation, students, or coworkers the importance you place on the message.

Friday is my day off and the members of my congregation know it. I've never announced it publicly; they tell one another. If I get a call on my day off and I can deal with the person's request quickly and simply, I do. Such requests are almost always preceded by,

"Pastor, I know this is your day off, but it would really help if ..." If someone asks me to go somewhere or do something out of the ordinary, I ask if it can wait until tomorrow. If it can't, I go. If there is an emergency, I'm there immediately.

The people of God are good. We can trust them. When they know our personal and family needs, they are only too happy to see that those needs are met. When the people we serve see us conscientiously caring for our families but also ready and available to serve them, they are less likely to question how we spend our free time. They trust us and honor our time-management decisions. In fact, I've learned that I get to know people better by honoring my personal and family commitments. Let me explain. Our children are involved in community activities, Scouts, sports, music, etc. When we attend the associated functions, we spend time with church members—delightful time, light-hearted time, time when we share the joy of victory and the sorrow of defeat. We bond on a wonderful level.

Family time involves much more than just kid/parent activities. It includes private time with your spouse. Although I've never done this myself, a friend and his wife have come up with a wonderful way to spend time together. The call it their "day away." They send their children off to school, jump into the car, and take off. To where? To the local Holiday Inn. They check into the hotel and spend a day together away from outside forces. They often pack a picnic lunch, and he may bring a video to watch while she enjoys a book. Although they are only a few miles from home, this change of venue gives them the feeling that they are far away. It enhances their conversation by removing the interruptions. As they step off life's treadmill and enjoy each other's company, they rediscover why they married. Sometimes they spend the night; most often they don't. A mini-vacation is all they need to recharge their batteries and re-enter the race.

I've found that an effective way to do business with church members is to meet for lunch. While not a formal setting, it is a special setting that enhances our ability to speak. Jesus put the time He spent "breaking bread" with His disciples to good use. I believe we can too. But why meet only my church members for lunch? Why not do it with family members too? Most schools, parochial or public, will allow parents to take their child off campus for lunch. I do this as often as I can. Sometimes it's one child, sometimes I take the whole tribe (four children is a tribe!). It's nothing fancy—any hamburger stand will do—but it gives us the chance to catch up with one another. And frankly, it makes children whose church worker parents don't always get to dance reviews and music recitals feel special.

If you do a good job of making time in your busy schedule for your family, congratulations. You are a blessing to them and to us. But if you aren't making time for your family, there's no better time than the present to repent and ask God to guide your time-management decisions. You are a blessing to your family, and by God's design, they need you. The people of God will understand your desire to be a blessing for your family. Ask God to make you bold enough to change. But remember, change comes slowly. So keep your goal, God's goal, before you. And ask Him to strengthen you to say yes to family and personal time.

To indicate my willingness to repent, I made this promise to my daughter Rebecca: "Rebecca, I didn't make your birth, but I promise to be there when you have your first child." To keep this promise, I'll need to take good care of myself. One of the best ways to take care of myself is to take care of my family.

PRAYER

Father, our families are Your special gifts to us, exceeded in sweetness only by the gift of Your Son. Enable us to look after our families in the same way You look after us. Help us to number our days and rejoice in each moment we spend with our families. Forgive us for Jesus' sake for those times we place our ministry before our families. Strengthen us for the tough time-management decisions and give all of us understanding spirits. In Jesus' name. Amen.

4

FISHBOWL EFFECT

One hot Saturday afternoon while cutting my lawn, I perspired so much that I'm sure I lost a couple pounds. After finishing my task, I was hot and tired. I decided to get some beer to cool down. I drove to the grocery store, got my beer, and stood in the checkout line. I was dirty and sweaty and not really ready to see anyone.

I think it was right in the middle of a prayer that no one I knew would come into the store that I felt someone tugging on my arm. I turned around and saw a woman I didn't recognize. She looked at me and asked, "Aren't you Reverend Rogers from the Lutheran church?" I answered yes. "Then what are you doing buying beer?" she asked. I think the shocked look on my face convinced her that I had been raised in a Christian tradition different than hers. (She was a member of the local nondenominational church, but her children had attended our vacation Bible school.) To vindicate myself, I quoted every appropriate Bible reference I could remember: "What goes into a man's mouth does not make him 'unclean,' but what comes out of his mouth." I quoted the apostle Paul's words to Timothy: "Stop drinking only water, and use a little wine because of your stomach and your frequent illnesses." And of course: "Do not judge, or you too will be judged." These did no good. Her parting words were that she was glad her children weren't with her to see me sin in such a public way.

I felt bad for the rest of the day. I didn't intend to offend the woman; I was just thirsty. If I thought I felt bad on Saturday, I was wrong—it got worse on Sunday. That's when I discovered that half the congregation had heard about my Saturday beer purchase. Most members who spoke to me thought it was amusing. They said they felt better knowing that I was being so closely scrutinized that I wouldn't dare get into trouble. I didn't find the situation quite so amusing. I didn't feel bad just because my life had been criticized. I felt bad because my life was on display. That means I'm open to criticism all the time. As professional church workers, our lives are always on display. As we do our jobs, we become well-known in our communities, and people will be watching.

Watching is fine, but judging isn't. Judgment is always subjective. This woman found me behaving beneath my office because I bought beer. Others would have acquitted me. Some would have celebrated the "humanness" my purchase revealed, which many say church workers lack. I dare say that if you went to a restaurant, ordered a steak, and then were served an unacceptable meal that you tried to send back, some people would tell the world that you had made a scene. I would further suggest that if you are shopping with your children and they become tired and cranky and cause a scene in the store, you and your children probably will be judged more severely than any other family. The age-old assessment is true: Church workers and their families live in fishbowls.

It would be very easy to lament this condition. Some have allowed this situation to drive them from their professions. But we don't need to resign. Instead, we can rejoice with the early disciples that we also have been deemed "worthy of suffering for the Name" of Jesus. We can look forward to letting the people we serve look directly into our fishbowls and not being scandalized but blessed.

The fishbowl can be an important ministry tool. It helps us help people grow in their discipleship. I don't mean that we should be perfect all the time. We do not have to provide a superhuman model for others to emulate. Rather, I'm suggesting that we can announce and display the essence of Christianity—Christians *aren't* perfect, but they *are* forgiven. If our life in the fishbowl can enable others to forgive themselves, their families, and those around them, then we have brought honor and glory to Christ.

I can't remember the issue, but sometime back I was arguing with my wife. The quiet but firm statements gave way to louder and firmer statements that gave way quite quickly to what must have looked like an out-of-control, screaming man. The screaming didn't last long, but it lasted long enough to upset my whole family. Once I calmed down, I realized what I had done. I saw the evil I had brought into our family. I lamented not only that I had lost my temper but that I had lost my temper in front of my children. I quickly called the whole family together and asked for their forgiveness. They looked into the fishbowl of their father's life and saw he was soiled and dirty. They also saw their father anxious to rid himself of that guilt. They heard me ask for forgiveness. I received it. I believe my children saw a model of behavior that they can and will emulate. We all are sinful human beings, therefore, we must learn how to repent and how to forgive. Our fishbowl existence becomes a blessing to us and the church as we demonstrate to the people we serve the ability to ask for and give forgiveness.

For years the young people of a church I once served were basically ignored by the congregation. They loved the young people, but they didn't pay much attention to what they did. That changed when these young people welcomed a young black man into the midst of this all-white congregation. This powerful stand for Christ got people's attention. The congregation started to examine everything the young people did, particularly what the young man did. He had absolutely no chance of getting away with the evil he perpetrated. One Sunday morning as the congregation moved to the chancel for Holy Communion, this young man moved through the pews and stole purses that had been left behind. He was caught, and the police arrested him. The church members were only too happy to prosecute the young man to the full extent of the law. Because he was a juvenile, he was released and returned home.

Because of their efforts to include this young man in their fellowship, the young people jumped into a fishbowl. The "fish" watchers observed an incident that confirmed their view that African-Americans should not belong to *their* church. They repeated this story again and again.

But the fishbowl kids more than withstood the scrutiny. You see, they took their visibility seriously. They knew that they were witnesses for Christ. In regard to this young man, they did the Christ-like thing and welcomed him back. They made sure that I went to his home to reassure his parents that we, as a church, welcomed them and their son. The kids made sure that I made clear to this family that we as a church don't just proclaim forgiveness for Jesus' sake but also live forgiveness.

These young people were so bold in their fishbowl that they elected their fallen friend treasurer of their youth group. In all my years in ministry, I don't believe that I have ever witnessed a more touching moment than when this young man came forward with the other youth group officers to be installed. The adults were humbled by their children. The fishbowl was a blessing.

The fishbowl is also a blessing for us if we understand that we are naturally sinful and unclean and will disappoint some people. The question of whether a church worker will fail is never a question of if, it is simply a question of when. We all have sinned and so fall short of the kingdom of God. That is a given. Therefore, we don't have to become upset or embarrassed if others speak out against the way we use our time, spend our money, treat our spouse, deal with our children, establish our tithe, or care for our family. Have we done a perfect job? No, not at all. We rightfully deserve criticism. But we know that we are forgiven.

Because we are forgiven by God for Jesus' sake, we can be quick to confess our sins, quick to ask for forgiveness, quick to take off our protective masks of supposed perfection and be who we are—forgiven children of God. Jesus has set us free from guilt and shame and worry. We will be who we are. And in so doing we will assist the Holy Spirit in setting a lot of people free from their guilt and shame.

A church member who hears his pastor confess to receiving a speeding ticket and then promise to amend his sinful, speedy life will be better able to forgive his wife or himself for a ticket. When a principal loses his or her temper in a meeting but asks the same assembly for forgiveness, he blesses the congregation. He makes it easier for a mother to ask forgiveness of her children when she falsely accuses them.

The devil intends the fishbowl in which we live to be a tomb. The devil wants the fishbowl to confine us, to frighten us, to take away any sense of spontaneity, creativity, or enthusiasm because of fear of what people might think or say. Remember what our Lord did to tombs—He broke out of them. He has broken us out of our tomb. Our behavior, when covered by a healthy spiritual life that can readily ask for forgiveness and offer a sincere promise to change, can break other people out of their tombs too.

Jesus told us that if we follow Him, we must take His "yoke" upon us because "[His] yoke is easy and [His] burden is light." And this statement is particularly true about the fishbowl. Holding the hand of our risen Lord, we fit ourselves and our families into the fishbowl knowing that it represents opportunities for joyful service, not a confining space that might swallow us.

Don't be afraid of the fishbowl. Instead, live boldly, giving thanks to God that He has found us worthy of the privilege of a fishbowl existence.

PRAYER

Father, we worry about living in a fishbowl. We worry because our water is dirty. Remind us that our dirty water is cleansed by Your Son's death and resurrection. Strengthen us so that, living in Your grace, we can be a blessing to Your people. In Jesus' name. Amen.

5

PERSONAL TIME

Church workers often find themselves in exhausting situations—physically, spiritually, and emotionally exhausting situations. Helping an obviously dysfunctional family to see what they need to do to help their child in school can wear you out. As a professional, you have to remain in control. Your words, although firm and clear, need to be spoken in loving tones. When your suggestions are ignored, you can feel extremely frustrated. Those who work with teenagers repeatedly try to speak the truth to young people who seem bent on doing only what is fun, exciting, pleasurable, or "hip," not what's right or healthy. Even when you get through to a young person, you might find yourself drained. Pastors often find themselves in the valley of the shadow of death. Often the valley is a well-furnished hospital room. Sometimes it's an emergency room. Occasionally, the valley is the side of the road.

All church workers come face to face with the power of sin, death, and the devil. Looking into the face of sin is like looking into the sun—we can only do it for a short period of time before it hurts us. We have to turn away to stay healthy. We have to turn away from the troubles and trials of ministry and refocus. We need to let our hair down. We have to get away to realize that there is a life out there worth living. Only then can we help others embrace this life. I know it's not easy to step outside our professional lives and relax. I found out the hard way.

I am an incurable sports fan. Baseball, football, basketball, lacrosse—I love them all. I attend sporting events whenever I get the opportunity. A friend who shares my zeal for sports and I bought season tickets for the New Orleans Saints. The football games usually took place on Sunday afternoons. On game days, I left church immediately after the second service and drove to the Superdome. Once there, it was as if I was in a different world. I didn't have to be reverent. I could cheer and high five people around me when my team did well. I could boo and complain when the referees made a bad call or our team failed to execute a play. I could eat a whole plate of nachos with jalapeno peppers and cool my throat with a fine Colorado beverage. No one passed judgment on my actions. People I didn't even know looked forward to seeing my friend and me appear at game time. We shook hands and told jokes with our neighboring season ticketholders. We formed a little family. After every game, win or lose, I left the stadium hoarse, exhausted, and happy.

All went well until the year the New Orleans Saints decided to stop their typical losing ways and win themselves into the play-offs—their first play-off experience in franchise history. The game was scheduled for noon Sunday instead of the regular 1 p.m. kickoff. The Sunday morning services which I conducted didn't end until 11:30 a.m., only 30 minutes before kickoff.

General Schwartzkopf would have been pleased with the plan of attack I developed to get to the football game on time. I asked a church member to be at the back door of the church at 11:30. I made sure my sermon was done on time (the congregation appreciated my brevity). At the end of the service, I stood before the congregation and said, "Folks, one of the high points of my week is greeting you after Sunday worship. This morning, I have an opportunity to do something else I enjoy. I have a ticket to the Saints' play-off game. If I'm going to make it, I'm going to have to leave now. Please let this be my greeting to you, and I'll look forward to spending more time with you next week." To my amazement, the congregation applauded, and I ran out. The acolyte was ready to take my vestments, which I ripped off in true Superman-in-the-phone-booth fashion. I jumped into my friend's car and was on my way. The people I served were happy. I was happy.

I got to the stadium and worked myself to my seat. I didn't have the time or a place to change my clothes so I appeared at my seat, a seat I had held for the entire football season, in my clergy shirt and collar. Even though the environment of a football game is generally excited and enthusiastic, when I arrived, those around me sat in silence. They couldn't believe their eyes. The fellow who had been cheering, booing, high-fiving, nacho-eating, and Colorado-beverage drinking was a clergyman. How could that be? I greeted everyone like I always did. I even took off my collar, but the breach had been made. I would never be the same in their eyes.

This event represents the tension we live with as professional church workers. People tell us to relax, spend time doing things away from the job, but the methods others use to relax and get away from it all, how others have fun, aren't always available to us. We can't erase the double standard. Others can be boisterous as they enjoy free time, but those of us who serve the church need to be more subdued.

I'm not sure the church is served when its workers defiantly stand against a common belief. I believe lasting change takes time and patience. However, in this instance, I make an exception. Professional church workers need to go out and let their hair down. It's all right to laugh and laugh loudly. It's all right to eat too much (once in a while). You and I won't do any harm to our Lord or His church if we act crazy or let our hair down.

Jesus knew that. He made it His business to have dinner with His friends, including Mary, Martha, and Lazarus. They seemed to provide Him with a safe place to enjoy His life. Jesus made it His business to attend weddings. His first miracle took place at a wedding. Jesus seems to have enjoyed Himself at appropriate times and suffered criticism because of it. Consider these words of Jesus:

> For John came neither eating nor drinking, and they say, "He has a demon." The Son of Man came eating and drinking, and they say, "Here is a glutton and a drunkard, a friend of tax collectors and 'sinners!' " (*Matthew 11:18–19*)

Jesus may have been criticized, but He didn't alter His lifestyle. He didn't stop having a good time just because others took offense at what He was doing. Jesus knew that, despite appearances to the contrary, His Father was in charge of the world so He could celebrate.

We all need to learn this lesson, and we get to— from our Lord. There is nothing wrong with celebrating, in fact, we practically have a mandate because of everything our Lord Jesus has secured for us. I grew up in a church where we sang a wonderful song immediately after the sermon. I always sang it with great gusto and joy, not because I was glad that I had caught the essence of the sermon but because I was glad the sermon had finally ended. Although I misunderstood the truth of the song's statement, "Restore to me the joy of Your salvation" (Psalm 51:12), its truth is still evident. We get to be joyful because of all God has done for us. All God's children, even professional church workers, have a right to celebrate the joy of their salvation. We express that joy in laughter, in lightheartedness, and sometimes in silliness. That's nothing new for the people of God, even King David got silly when the ark of the covenant was brought back to Zion. David danced, danced mightily, danced delightedly, before the Lord.

You and I have been given the same privilege to dance before the Lord. Some of us literally dance for joy when we celebrate. Others go to ball games and yell and scream for joy. Some sing for joy in choirs and performing groups or celebrate by planting and tending gardens. Others celebrate with a good book that makes them happy or sad. Still others run, swim, sail, hike, or jump out of airplanes. All these expressions of joy are perfect ways to honor God and celebrate His good gifts.

So when was the last time you had a really great time? When was the last time you had a blast? If your answer is more than a week ago, then you owe God a good time. Go out and enjoy yourself. Our Lord will rejoice in the fact that you are rejoicing in the joy of your salvation.

PRAYER

Father, we live in your loving and forgiving presence. Remind us of Your creative, celebrative side. Encourage us as we find new ways to express our joy in Your gift of salvation and even some silly ways to celebrate the many gifts You have given us. May our laughter, joy, and silliness bless Your people and bring You joy. In Jesus' name. Amen.

6

LAUGHTER IN THE VINEYARD

Our church's sacristy is too small. Built more than 30 years ago when the congregation had 100 members, its counter, sink, and cupboards provided copious space for preparing once-a-month communion for the flock.

But things have changed. Our congregation now has 2,000 members, and we own significantly more communionware. And sometime since 1960, banners caught on at our church. They're stored in the sacristy until their appointed time. Three full-time pastors and two part-time pastors serve the congregation—all of whom store their vestments, stoles, and suit jackets in the sacristy. The sacristy holds altar flowers that await transportation to a hospital or nursing home after Sunday services. Leftover vases, kneeling rails, and confirmation textbooks left by absent-minded acolytes add to the sacristy's clutter. To top it all off, about 20 years ago the congregation showed its appreciation for its pastors by constructing a men's room. You guessed it. It's in the sacristy.

While our church's sacristy may be small, it constantly teaches us what is truly sacred and how sacred things often take us by surprise. For example, one summer Sunday I entered the sacristy hot and tired. Preaching three services in an unair-conditioned building had taken its toll on my body. I worked my way past the absent-minded acolyte who was removing his robe and about to forget his catechism. I tried to slide my less-than-slender body through the assembly line of ladies who were carefully cleaning the sacred vessels. After a few bumps and a few my-sin-is-ever-before-me stories about my weight, I found myself standing before the closet where I would "divest" myself of my alb and cool down. Opening the closet, I discovered that the acolyte didn't know how a hanger works. I hung up his alb and then my own as I listened to the busy conversation of the altar guild ladies. They were comparing the virtues of plastic individual cups to the traditional glass individual cups.

Still hot and tired, I sought sanctuary in … the rest room. As I washed my face, I heard concerned voices: "We're all done except for these six unused cups of wine." Then I heard the voice of one of our ever-faithful ladies: "You all go ahead. I'll take care of it." As I dried my face, I thought of how grateful the Lord must be for those who go above and beyond the call of duty like this dear lady who was emptying the six cups. The frantic voice of our associate pastor broke in on my musings. "Eloise!" he cried. Eloise is 88 years old, so I ran into the room as fast as I could, fully expecting to see that Eloise had met her Lord.

Well, she had met her Lord but not in the way I thought. Eloise saw no use in pouring the wine on the ground, so instead she drank it, one cup at a time. When I arrived on the scene (it was a short trip), the associate pastor exclaimed again, "Eloise, you're drinking the communion wine!"

The associate pastor looked shook up. Eloise looked embarrassed. Something pastoral needed to be said, so I lifted my voice and said, "Eloise, you are drinking the communion wine. You should know there is a two-tray limit around here." After a moment of unsure and embarrassed silence, everyone laughed. A deep shade of red covered all three of us and accompanied the laughter. Eloise turned red because she had been caught "red-handed" as she disposed of the leftover communion wine. The associate pastor was embarrassed because he had "overreacted." I was embarrassed because I thought I may have underreacted to this indiscretion. Feeling each other's embarrassment, we embraced, apologized, laughed, and held on to one another.

Of all the times I've been in our sacristy, I don't believe I've ever seen the presence of the Almighty more clearly or more wonderfully. There we were—three sinners laughing at our reactions. The masks, offices, or mystique that might have hidden and separated us were gone. Naked in our sin, we were fleeing to God's infinite mercy, seeking and imploring His grace. We each knew His grace and forgiveness were ours so we could laugh, even laugh at ourselves.

It was a lighthearted moment in the sacristy, but a solemnly sacred moment as well. Sinners were rejoicing in the presence of their Savior. In the face of a world and a church that too often insists we "straighten up" or "take this more seriously" or "be still and don't play around," three people relished the joy of their salvation and didn't take themselves seriously. I'm sure we weren't just a rollicking threesome but a raucous foursome. We laughed at our futility and rejoiced in our forgiveness, and God, I believe, giggled too. He giggled because we didn't take ourselves seriously. That must make Him happy because it demonstrates that we know He is the Creator and we are His creatures. He is the Almighty, and we are His needy children. Once we know that, there will be no more towers of Babel, no more scribes or Pharisees, no more self-righteous, slogan-tossing hypocrites. It makes God happy because we understand that our salvation doesn't depend on our performance. We can relax and rejoice.

So try it: Find your communion wine-guzzling (in moderation) Grandma and laugh about it. Such a wondrous woman may not exist in your fellowship, but I'm sure that someone among you (maybe you yourself) can remind people that we're unbelievably human, not blasphemously divine.

Thank God for and celebrate the dear secretary whose word processing mistake leads us to believe we are worshiping on January 15, *1895*. Bless the same secretary who in printing that great Easter hymn leaves out a *g* so that the entire congregation sings, "Where the angels ever *sin*, Alleluia."

Thank God for the young confirmand who, when asked to recite the meaning of the Tenth Commandment, nervously said, "We should fear and love God so that we do not covet our neighbor's manservant or his maidservant, his mistress ..." (It took 10 minutes to settle the congregation down.) Thank God for the parents who cringe as their son shakes the pastor's hand and says, "My dad says he sleeps good when you talk."

Thank God for all of them. They remind us that laughter directed at ourselves is holy, and it lifts God on high. Thank God for those who help us to not take ourselves seriously but to take God very seriously. While we're at it, thank God for His Son, Jesus, whom He sent to free us from our sin. And maybe God could see to it that our sacristies will never be too small.

PRAYER

Father, may we trust so powerfully in Your love and sovereignty that we may laugh with one another and at ourselves when we stumble as we work in Your Kingdom. In Jesus' name. Amen.

7

MONEY AND MINISTRY

During her first year in high school, our eldest daughter played on the freshman volleyball team. She had a great time. At season's end, I asked her if she planned to try out for the varsity squad her sophomore year. "Probably not," she answered, catching me by surprise. I had watched her play, and she was good, at least as good as the other players. I asked the favorite parental question, "Why not?" My eyes opened further when she replied, "These girls will be much better than me by next year." Wanting to bolster what I considered a sagging sense of self-esteem, I said, "Elizabeth, you're getting better every day. By this time next year, you'll be able to hold your own with anyone." She gave me that "I love you, Dad, but you're so naive" look and said, "Daddy, these girls will play 'club' volleyball this summer. They'll play every day, and next year, they'll be tremendously improved. Club volleyball makes you very, very good."

Club volleyball is an organization of volleyball enthusiasts. They form leagues made up of better-than-average volleyball players coached by better-than-average coaches whose goal it is to get college volleyball scholarships for the players. When Elizabeth said her friends would get better because they would play club volleyball, I said, "Then, Elizabeth, you'll play club volleyball." She gave me another "I love you, Dad, but you are so naive" look and said, "Daddy, I can't. The registration fee is $2,500, and that doesn't count uniforms and other fees."

I'm not speechless often, but I was then. I was in a state of shock. I wasn't surprised and shocked just because a club volleyball team membership was so expensive. I was shocked that my daughter had so accurately figured out her place in life. She knew that even though my salary as a pastor has been supplemented by my wife's salary as a Christian teacher, we still haven't made enough money for her to do what her peers can do.

Financial issues weren't much of a problem when our children were young, but it's become more obvious as they've gotten older. Our children's friends are the children of doctors, engineers, bankers, business owners, and the like. These are the very people whose family crises cut into the time I can spend with my children on Sunday afternoons.

My kids are aware that the reason I couldn't attend their dance recital was that I was officiating at their best friend's mother's remarriage. They know how many times I've missed back-to-school nights because I'm conducting Bible class. They've gotten used to my absence at major events in their lives because I'm officiating at or ministering to the major events in their friends' lives. They've heard my car leave in the middle of the night numerous times and have prayed that God would send angels to protect me without knowing where I was headed. They know we live with and are an important part of their friends' families' lives, but they don't enjoy the same privileges as their friends. Yes, their friends' parents who are doctors put in long, unusual hours. Yes, their friends' parents who are lawyers work long hours and sometimes miss family celebrations. But even at such a young age, my kids know that their friends' parents receive much larger salaries for their long hours than I do.

All of us who have been called by our Lord into full-time service in the church can tell the same story. Some of us have even told our stories to the church's leadership in an attempt to alert them to financial reality. Many of those brothers and sisters can presently be found selling fraternal insurance. What are we to make of all this? Directors of Christian education, principals, teachers, deaconesses, and pastors are generally highly intelligent, well-educated people. I've repeatedly heard church workers say, "I could make a lot more money in the private sector." But we know that church workers' salaries probably will never equal what people make in the secular work place for similar jobs, skills, or education level. What are we to do?

Several options leap to mind. We could form a union and stand together for better pay. I'd like to suggest a couple names for our union. The first name is OLSER, which stands for *O*rganized *C*hurch *L*eaders *S*triving to *E*qualize *R*emuneration and is pronounced *ulcer.* A second suggestion is LOSERS, which stands for Church Leaders Organized to See to It That Everyone Has a Respectable Salary, commonly called *losers*. I believe those names prophesy the success of such organizations. If the unions fail, we could just gather in teachers' lounges, DCE clusters, and pastors' conferences and gripe and complain about our poor treatment. Another option would be to follow the advice my first boss gave me when I tried to get a raise from $1.05 to $1.25 an hour. He said, "Son, if you don't like it, don't complain … quit."

But no matter how frustrated or desperate we become, none of the above are God-pleasing options. "What are God-pleasing options?" you ask. The real question is, "Where are God-pleasing options found?" As always, in the Scriptures. Consider 1 Timothy 6:7–8, a word from a seasoned church worker to a young church worker:

> For we brought nothing into the world, and we can take nothing out of it. But if we have food and clothing, we will be content with that.

Although these words speak powerfully to those of us who are privileged to serve the Lord publicly, they are primarily directed to all Christians. God wants all His people—teachers, preachers, deaconesses, DCEs, doctors, lawyers, and candlestick makers—to enjoy such peace in Him that they can say, "If we have food and clothing, we will be content with that." God forgive me for the paraphrase, but I think our Lord is suggesting that each of us should live so as to consume as little as we can of what the Lord has given us and give the greatest part away.

49

Can you imagine what the church could do to spread the Gospel of Christ if a doctor who earns $200,000 a year lived on $40,000 and gave the rest to the church for the Lord's work? What if a contractor who made $350,000 chose to live on $30,000 and gave the rest to the Lord who saved him from sin, death, and the power of the devil? What ministry could be accomplished if a pastor who was paid $50,000 would strive to live on $35,000 and would let the Holy Spirit have total access to the rest!

If such were the case, foreign missions would grow. Church bodies wouldn't have to make the agonizing decision about which mission fields to work in and which to leave unstaffed or understaffed. If all those who have been "baptized into Christ's death" die also to personal desires and give to Jesus all they can, new missions could begin all across this country. Then students preparing for professional church work could graduate debt free. Then those who want to enter the ministry as a second career but who don't want to incur $50,000 of debt for a job that pays $20,000 could do so confidently.

But how will people ever be convinced that they can do such great things for the Lord? Probably only one way—by example. Brothers and sisters, it is wonderful that God has called us to be His witnesses and to set an example for others. Our reward will not be found here where rust, moths, inflation, fire, taxes, and children who need extra-special help to get started can destroy it. Instead, our reward will be in heaven.

The devil wants us to believe that our personal sacrifices will do no good. He continually shows us that our faithfulness doesn't change anyone. The devil wants us to look out for ourselves. But Jesus reminds us we are a part of this ministry for the long haul, not for the short run. Our actions may not affect this generation, but they could affect a future generation.

The privilege of serving the Lord and making sacrifices for the sake of the kingdom helps our children grow up in many special ways. The children of church workers know what's important and what's not. They seem to find their place in the world more easily than self-centered kids. And they don't seem to miss out on a single thing.

By the way, Elizabeth gave up volleyball and started running cross country. She was rookie of the year!

PRAYER

Father, help us to be content with what You have given us. Make us more committed to giving away more than we ever believed we could. In Jesus' name. Amen.

8

FORGIVENESS AND THE PROFESSIONAL CHURCH WORKER

One Sunday morning, a mother took me aside. She told me that her 13-year-old son had stolen a fellow student's lunch money and had been suspended from school. She asked me to speak to him. I called him into my office and told him that I understood that he had had a really tough week. He agreed and then explained what had happened. When he finished, I asked him how he felt. The young man said he felt awful. He knew he had done something wrong, and he was sorry for his actions and for the embarrassment he had caused his family. After several seminary classes on the distinction between Law and Gospel, I knew it was time to speak the Gospel to this repentant soul. So I told him he was forgiven by God, and as far as I was concerned, my feelings about him had not changed a bit, even though I knew about his sin. We hugged, and he left.

The next Sunday, the same woman called me over and told me she couldn't believe what I had said to her son. Knowing that kids don't always pass on to their parents exactly what they've heard, I asked her what her son had told her. "He said you told him that he was forgiven," she said incredulously. She had expected me to come down hard on the lad and tell him beyond a shadow of a doubt that God was not pleased with what he had done. She wanted me to tell her son that if he continued on this present path, he would lose all hope of a happy earthly life and heaven as well. The family left our church.

I can understand the woman's disappointment. She was frightened by what her son had done and hoped I would help straighten her son out. But the woman and I (frankly, the woman and Jesus) have two different ideas about how that straightening out happens. Desperate for a quick change in her son's behavior, she thought her goal could be achieved with threat and force. Jesus is convinced that the only way people change is through a change of heart. A change of heart comes not through threats but through love. Jesus is right.

Our task as professional church workers is to proclaim the forgiveness of sins to repentant sinners. We are sent into ministry to love people into forgiveness. I believe the ability to forgive is the critical factor in determining the success of our ministries. That's important for us to keep in mind. In the heat of ministry, when disrespectful children and lethargic, apathetic parents and adults are everywhere, it's easy to come down hard with nothing but words of judgment. Such a reaction doesn't grow the church, it kills it. I know. I almost killed one.

The first parish I served had been planted in a quickly growing section of New Orleans. District officials were so confident in the success of this mission that the mission developer allowed the congregation to build a full-size gymnasium. The church began with about 200 people in worship. The future looked bright. But then the U.S. space program began to wane. The church had attracted many employees of the space program and now the newly formed congregation was forced to say good-bye to half of its members. What remained was a huge debt on the property and the gymnasium, which the congregation worshiped in for more than 25 years. A few years after I arrived, the congregation decided to develop the school it had long planned to start. God blessed the school and made it a wonderful success. Before long, it became clear that the congregation would have to build a permanent sanctuary.

We raised money, drew up plans, and began construction. As pastor, it was a tremendous joy to see the gratitude and amazement on the faces of the members who had been waiting for this day for more than two decades. The Lord was working mightily among us. And so was the devil. You see, throughout my seminary training and in conversations with trained church musicians, I learned that "real" churches had wonderful acoustics. A truly God-pleasing sanctuary was designed to make singing sound angelic and organ playing sound divine. I'm no musician, but I had been taught that good acoustics required hard surfaces in the building and a modicum of padding and carpeting.

Whenever the subject of carpeting and pews came up in the building committee meetings, I would mount my pulpit and plead with the people to install tile instead of carpet and to make sure that the pews were all hardwood with no padding. After visiting the issue several times, we agreed to a compromise. There would be carpet up the center aisle but only up the center aisle. There would be padding on the pews but only on the seats. With that decision firmly in place, we called in a pew builder.

Located as we were in the southern Bible Belt, members of the Southern Baptist church were everywhere, including in the pew building business. A member of the building committee and I traveled to northern Louisiana to meet this Southern Baptist pew builder and make clear to him what sort of pew we wanted. As we toured his factory, we made it clear that we wanted a pew that was padded only on the seat. He repeatedly mentioned that such a pew was expensive and hard to make. We acknowledged his concerns, but we still wanted hardbacked pews. We even explained the reason— the acoustics.

The pew builder said he would come to New Orleans, meet with the building committee, and sign the contract. We established a meeting time and returned to New Orleans, rejoicing in our accomplishment and dreaming about the quality of sound we would enjoy in our brand new sanctuary.

When the appointed time arrived, the pew builder met with the building committee. We spent about a half hour going through the details of the project. We restated our desire for hardback pews. We heard again the pew builder's suggestion that we could save money and time by buying fully padded pews. We thanked him for his concern but insisted he build to our specifications. He agreed. A price was set. A delivery date was set. Convinced that my work was over, I excused myself and made a hospital call.

Every day between that meeting and the arrival of the pews was exciting. Construction was winding down. The tile was installed, and it was glorious. The paneling in the church was installed, and it was beautiful. The center carpet runner was installed, and it was very nice. Each time I entered the sanctuary, I snapped my fingers and smiled as I heard the *snap* echo through the room. I smiled with pride. I was sure we had done what all my colleagues told me to do to build a sanctuary with good acoustics. The day before the pews arrived, the organ installation was completed. Our organist tested things out. She played a glorious hymn that filled the room with sounds of praise, and when she took her fingers off the keyboard after the last chord, the reverberation seemed to last a full minute! We all cheered. My dreams were all coming true. We spent the evening making sure everything was ready for the pew installers who were scheduled to come the next day. I went to bed a very happy man.

The next afternoon, the pew installers pulled into the church's parking lot in huge trucks full of beautiful pews. My heart was pounding. We were just a few hours away from completing our building project. I went out to greet the foreman of the crew. We exchanged pleasantries, and then he opened the first truck to reveal the pews—the *fully* padded pews. My jaw dropped. My blood pressure rose. I told the foreman that there had been a tremendous mistake and that he should not take a single pew off that truck.

Seething with every step, I entered my office and called the Southern Baptist pew builder from Northern Louisiana. When I got him on the phone, I told him that he had violated our contract, and I was sending the trucks back. We would have to call a special meeting of the building committee to see whether we wanted him to build the correct pews.

I could hear him grinning on the other end of the phone. He said, "Brother Rogers, you get your copy of the contract and see if I haven't done just what it called for." I asked my secretary to find our copy, and there, right before my eyes, I saw that he was supposed to build a whole sanctuary full of *fully* padded pews. "This isn't the contract we agreed to" I protested. "This isn't the contract *you* agreed to, but it is the contract your people agreed to. The minute you left that meeting, I told those people you didn't know what you were talking about. I told them that pews had nothing to do with acoustics and that all your obsession with hard surfaces was doing was costing them money. They agreed with me, we rewrote the contract and saved your church $20,000. You should thank me," he replied in a somewhat surly tone.

I now understand how crimes of passion take place. I was filled with blind rage. Right then and there I called every member of the building committee at home or at work. I spoke to each person for at least five minutes. I'm sure that each sentence began with, "How dare you?" Several times during each phone call, I slammed my hand down hard on my desk. My secretary couldn't believe what she was seeing. The formerly mild-mannered pastor had become a raving lunatic.

After making my phone calls, I walked around the lake that was next to the church's property. After about the second revolution, I could see a crowd was beginning to gather. The word was out that pastor was mad. I walked by this crowd of curious onlookers three times before I said a word to them. I felt that if I opened my mouth again, I would say something that I would really regret. As I walked, I grieved. I grieved over what I knew would be the loss of tremendous acoustics (which unfortunately proved to be the case). I grieved over what I perceived to be the loss of the pastoral relationship between myself and the people. They had lied to me. They had ignored me. Worse, they thought me a detriment to their ministry.

Finally, I stopped and exchanged a few words with the people who by now were walking around trying to stay busy. With just the exchange of a few words, I could tell that something horrible was happening. A building that was being built to the glory of God, a building that was supposed to be a monument to the Most High God, was becoming a monument to hatred, anger, and division.

There was no doubt I was hurt. I could not understand how the congregation could allow something like this to happen. But I recalled something else. I was the pastor. I am to be a model of the godly life. I wasn't modeling anything but a selfish, anger-driven attitude. I asked the Lord to forgive me and to empower me to forgive everyone else involved in this debacle, including the Southern Baptist pew builder from Northern Louisiana. Thanks be to God, the grace was given. He would not allow a project intended to bring so much good to His people to do them so much harm just because I didn't get my way. Although the praise offered to God wouldn't bounce around the hardwood walls for as long as I had hoped, it would bounce off the walls of heaven just as wonderfully as if they had installed "my" pews. The glorious sacraments would continue to convey the forgiveness of sins to God's people even if there was a lot more padding than I wanted.

I called every member of the building committee back. I apologized and asked for their forgiveness. To my surprise, they offered the same words to me, "Please forgive me, and let's go on from here." A lot of tears were shed, and a lot of hugs were exchanged. Three days later, we dedicated the building.

On the day of the dedication, I thanked God for the whole unfortunate circumstance. As a result of the pew mishap, our congregation received a marvelous lesson in why we exist. We were reminded that we are here to proclaim and demonstrate the forgiveness of sins. To the extent that we forgive, the church grows and flourishes. To the extent that the church is not able to forgive sins, it withers.

I believe that God has placed the mantle of forgiveness on the shoulders of professional church workers. That is, we are charged to be examples of forgiveness. It breaks my heart to hear stories of pastors, teachers, deaconesses, and DCEs who are at loggerheads with their congregations. The reasons for the impasses are usually not theological, rather they revolve around pure, unadulterated pride. Some pastors believe that an admission of fault or guilt on their part might compromise their position in the congregation. Teachers who refuse to apologize for an indiscretion often fear the loss of parental respect. DCEs sometimes lose youth group members because they won't back down out of fear of losing respect. But the opposite usually occurs. Admissions, apologies, and a servant attitude will elevate church workers in the minds and hearts of those we serve. When church workers are so filled with the love of Christ that they care about the condition of His church more than they care about their reputations, God is exalted. When we ask for forgiveness, God is glorified. The church grows, and the church worker grows in the eyes of the flock he or she serves.

To this very day, the people of God at that church in New Orleans look upon their sanctuary with thanks and tell great stories about it. They proudly describe how they raised money and paid off the construction costs within one year. They solemnly recall how the sanctuary cross was lifted into place prior to a Good Friday service while the whole congregation held flashlights and sang "Lift High the Cross." They discuss the hundreds of people who were present at the dedication. But the story they tell most frequently is about people of God, angry with one another, who were able, by the power of God, to put their differences behind them. They forgave one another, loved one another, and continued to work together in the kingdom of God.

Brothers and sisters in service to our Lord, recognize that you wear the mantle of forgiveness. Use it. Forgive, forgive, forgive, and forgive and watch your congregation grow in love and in size.

PRAYER

Lord, Your forgiveness is new to us every day. Thank You. Empower us to model forgiveness every day of our lives. In Jesus' name. Amen.

9

TIME OFF

Once upon a time, there was a pastor who worked hard day in and day out for his Lord and for the congregation he served. As best he could recall, it had been five years since his last day off. Tired and bedraggled, he dragged himself to a congregational meeting and asked for permission to take one day off each week. The congregational members began to speak to the issue. Some said it was a good idea. Others wondered if it showed proper commitment to the Lord's work. After about 30 minutes of discussion, an exasperated woman stood up and said, "Pastor, I can't understand how you, a man of God could even consider taking a day off. The devil doesn't ever take a day off." The pastor stood up and responded, "Yes, ma'am, that's true, and if I don't start taking a day off, I'll be just like him."

It's a silly story, but it is true. Church workers need to take time off. I didn't believe that for a time. I worked diligently and steadily at my ministry. I exulted when people told me I was working too hard. I believed their recognition of my efforts meant they loved and appreciated me. The more they seemed to love and appreciate me, the harder I worked, sacrificing my health and my family. One Easter Sunday, I worked my way back to my office about eight o'clock in the evening. At about ten o'clock, one of my best friends saw my car in the parking lot and stopped by the church. He came into the office, took one look at me laboring over some papers, and said, "Rogers, there's something I need to inform you of: The number of people who attend your funeral will be more a function of the weather than it will be of anything you accomplish in this life." I laughed, but I never really believed what he said … until.

It was a Monday morning. On Monday mornings, we always hold a staff meeting. The meeting was a little stressful but not out of the ordinary. I was a little surprised when I began to feel a pain, a strange pain. It started in my throat and began to move down toward my chest. Once it got into my chest, it began to radiate through my arms. I knew enough about chest pain to suspect that I might be in trouble. The more anxious I became, the more the pain intensified. But I had a staff meeting to run, and run it I did.

I finished the meeting and approached my secretary. "I'm sort of having pains in my chest," I said. "It's probably nothing, but just to make sure, would you mind driving me to the hospital?" She was kind enough to do so. She dropped me at the emergency room entrance, and I walked inside and spoke to the receptionist. When she asked if she could help me, I apologized for the inconvenience and said, "I've got a little pain in my chest." She excused herself and went through a door.

The next thing I heard was the crashing sound of someone running through double doors. The crash was made by a wheelchair, a wheelchair coming to get me. Two rather large men pushed me into the chair and wheeled me into the emergency room. They got me onto a bed, and four nurses began removing my clothing (without my permission, I might add!). They didn't seem to care about my feelings; they were solely concerned about my heart. The nurses placed electrocardiogram pads on my chest and drew blood from my arm. The preliminary results indicated I had suffered a heart attack. They wheeled me into the cardiac care unit, and I spent the rest of the day and night looking at my heartbeat on a monitor … and praying earnestly.

The next morning, a nurse drew a new blood sample and ran another electrocardiogram. The results indicated that I had not suffered a heart attack but had suffered a stress attack. I was released from the hospital and told to make an appointment with my new cardiologist. The cardiologist decided to conduct a Thallium cardiogram. The results indicated that despite the doctor's previous diagnosis of a stress attack, I probably had at least 60 percent blockage in the arteries leading to my heart. The cardiologist scheduled an angiogram to verify how much and where the blockages were. The test revealed no blockage to my heart. I breathed a sigh of relief and made enormous promises to myself and others to change my lifestyle. I would take it easier. I would get more rest.

As the days passed, I forgot my promises. In fact, as I reflected on the whole experience, I began to deny that anything could be wrong with my health, therefore, nothing could be wrong with my lifestyle. I particularly criticized the high-tech thallium EKG machine that could make such a costly error, an error that put me through the trauma of an angiogram. I complained to anyone who would listen and some who probably didn't want to listen. In my mind, my arguments further supported my position that I could work all I wanted without doing damage to myself.

My wife got tired of listening to my complaints. She told me I was being unfair to the doctors and the machines they used. I, of course, was defensive. "How can you say that? The facts speak for themselves. They made a mistake—I didn't have a blockage," I pointed out for the umpteenth time. "How do you know they made a mistake? You had a lot of people praying for you. The Lord may have chosen to heal you and give you a second chance to change your lifestyle," she quietly responded.

The wind went out of my sails. My attitude became one of humble thanksgiving. My efforts to act like a superman came to an end. I began to take time for myself. God got my attention. Now I'm praying that I won't make it necessary for Him to be so dramatic again.

I pray the same for you. Take your responsibility to rest and restore your vitality seriously. If fear of the consequences of overwork is not enough to make you change your lifestyle, then look at the life of our Lord. Jesus worked extremely hard but never so hard that He lost touch with what His body was telling Him. When Jesus became tired, He took time off. When Jesus had spent considerable time healing people or preaching and teaching, He would go to a quiet place, away from the people, to pray (Mark 1:35). When you read God's Word closely, you find that, even when still surrounded by people who needed Him, Jesus knew He had to retreat and rest and pray to His Father.

Imagine you live in New Testament times. You hear that Jesus is coming to your region—the Jesus who people claim can heal the sick. You have a brother who has been permanently injured, and he and his family have become a burden to your family. Neither you nor your brother, nor your families, can live as you want. You're all hampered with extra duties and frustrated. Jesus offers the chance for your brother to be healed. You construct a stretcher to carry him to Jesus.

When you finally find Jesus, you see that hundreds of people have the same idea as you. You take your place at the end of a line full of the blind, the lame, and the demon-possessed. While it's not a happy experience, you celebrate as each step brings you closer to Jesus. The praises coming from those already healed heightens your confidence and enthusiasm. Throughout the heat of the day, your faith that Jesus can heal your brother and thus turn everyone's lives around keeps you going.

Finally, Jesus is only a few feet away. Within a few minutes, your life, and your brother's, will be changed. You begin to sing praises to God. But Jesus stands up, heaves a great sigh, and walks away. His disciples announce that He is tired and must rest.

It would be easy to understand how people trapped in such a situation could become angry with Jesus. They could claim He was unfair and lacked sympathy or understanding of their situations. Some might even suggest that He didn't take His responsibilities seriously. If they could, I'm sure some would have fired Him.

Jesus was true God. He knew all things so He probably realized that bad feelings arose when He didn't help every family who had hoped He was the answer to their problems. Jesus might have been tempted to ignore His physical, mental, and yes, even spiritual exhaustion to keep ministering to the huge crowds. But He didn't. Jesus was also true man. He knew that this frail human body gets tired, that it needs rest. Jesus granted Himself time for relaxation, rest, and meditation. He took time to eat, and sleep, and most important, to talk with His Father.

Jesus gives us the same freedom. We can and must take time for ourselves. If we don't, chances are you will have fewer years to serve God, which only serves the interests of the evil one. Yes, some will begrudge you the time you spend recharging your batteries, but you can take the same posture our Lord did. To continue our ministries, we need to spend time alone with our Lord and time alone with our families. It's God pleasing to spend time enjoying ourselves and enjoying His creation.

I didn't enjoy my stay in the cardiac care unit. It was frightening and unnecessary. Ultimately, it was time that I didn't spend serving the Lord or His people. If I had spent small blocks of time over the years taking care of my physical, mental, and spiritual needs, I may not have needed such a rude wake-up call. Wise people learn from the experiences of others. I pray that you learn a lesson from me and others like me. If you would like to discuss this issue, call me anytime except Friday. That's my day off.

PRAYER

Lord Jesus, enable us to live our days at Your pace, not at our own hectic pace or at the urging of others. Encourage us to take advantage of times of rest. Remind us that we need to spend time on ourselves, our families, and especially with You. Forgive us for not being wise stewards of our time. In Your name we pray. Amen.

10

SELF-ESTEEM

Christopher and Andrew's parents are professional church workers. These two little boys have been coming to worship since before they could walk. Now that they're ages 5 and 3, they are so well versed in "doing church" that they have reenacted it at home. Their reenactment was much more perceptive than anyone could have imagined. Let me explain what I mean.

First, a little background information. I have few claims to fame, but I happen to be remarkable for one thing: I was one of the last people in California, for that matter the entire United States, to contract polio. I got it six months before the Salk vaccine became available to the public. By the grace of God, the only lasting effect is that my right leg is smaller and shorter then my left leg. That means I walk with a limp. It hasn't been too much of a liability. After all, I'm privy to the best parking places in town. While I'm as active as anyone, there are a few things I've never been able to do, such as ride a bike, run, and dance, which with my sense of rhythm is probably a blessing. Now back to Christopher and Andrew.

As I mentioned, they decided to reenact church at home. Christopher, the elder of the two, would preach to Andrew, and then they would trade places. The two boys got better and better at playing church and began to read lessons, pray prayers, and even take offerings. Their parents beamed with pride. As if home church that included an offering was not enough, the boys decided they would start having church with communion. They got some bread and some grape juice and began to reenact this important and sacred celebration. Watching their children do this great thing, the boys' mother and father beamed. However, their beams of pride turned to incredulous stares and then to laughter when they saw what the boys did next. Each child took turns kneeling to receive communion from the other. When it was his turn to "play" pastor, each boy approached the other, walking with a limp. When Christopher and Andrew's parents told me, we all roared with laughter.

I shared this story with the staff at church and with many friends. One friend provided a surprising commentary on the story when he said, "That's such a compliment to you." It threw me into a minor tailspin. You see, my polio-generated limp was never something I celebrated or viewed with thanksgiving. It certainly didn't seem to be something that anyone else would want to copy. But the copying the boys did indicated how Jesus, working in us, can enable us to overcome our handicaps and challenges and bring glory to Him.

Christopher and Andrew taught us a wonderful lesson. Our worth does not depend on our looks, gifts, talents, or skills. Instead, it totally depends on Christ working in us. And Christ promises to use all our deficiencies for His glory. (He did a great job with the man born blind. See John 9:11.)

Life wasn't much fun for me while I was growing up. Because of my leg, I couldn't participate in activities with the other kids, even though I had a burning desire to do so. Whether at school or the swimming pool, people just gawked at my legs or made fun of my gate. Through it all, my parents assured me that I was a special child of God. They promised me that God would turn my trouble into triumph. I trusted the truth of their word, and I trusted God.

Because I trusted my parents, I went to school and tried to behave like every other kid. When it came time to play football, basketball, or baseball during recess, I gathered with the other boys and waited to be picked. I would love to tell you that I was picked last every time. I would love to tell you that, but I can't. The truth is I was seldom picked at all. My classmates knew about my inabilities so the team that made the second-to-last pick would always say, "Now that leaves Rogers. You got him." The usual response was, "We don't need 'im. Let's play." No matter how many times I told myself that I wouldn't cry if I wasn't chosen, I did. And that meant I wasn't just unworthy to play ball, I was a wimp who cried in front of his "macho" classmates.

One day while I was in mid-sob, my second-grade teacher, Mrs. Kressin, paid me a visit. She put her arms around me and tried to comfort me. She asked me why I was so sad, and in an attempt to make a long story short (a tendency I gave up shortly after my ordination), I said, "I can't run." I'll never forget her response. She told me that although I may not be able to run, Jesus would

71

make it possible for me to fly. From her, I heard for the first time those powerful words from the prophet Isaiah, "They that wait upon the Lord shall renew their strength; they shall mount up with wings like eagles." I trusted her words and waited to see whether they would come true. Because of her words, I was able to do things I might not have done otherwise, like try out for a Little League team.

I will never forget the day of the tryouts. Boys packed our neighborhood playground, eager to show their ability. Enthusiasm and excitement ran high. One by one, we were called onto the diamond to field grounders, catch flies, and bat. Our performances were graded. Each time someone ran onto the field, his family and friends cheered. After what seemed an endless wait, my name was called. As I walked to my position, everyone was silent. There were no claps, no cheers, just quiet wonder and unspoken disbelief.

When everyone had been given their chance to try out, the coaches went into the park office to choose teams. Since I had never had much luck when teams were chosen, I was worried. At the end of the day, the results were posted outside the park director's office. I strained through the crowd of anxious boys to see if my name appeared on the roster of some team, any team. To my amazement, there it was, my name. I was a Brave. I looked to see the name of my coach—Mrs. Alice Tewlewski. I had a female baseball coach ... in 1963. Mrs. Tewlewski sought me out and told me she was happy to have me on her team. She said she had watched the way that I threw and she was pretty sure that I would be able to pitch. It was too good to be true.

Not only was I on a team, I was going to get to pitch. God had been good.

I arrived an hour early for our first practice, almost overwhelmed with excitement. I was so proud and happy to be on an organized baseball team that I didn't think twice when the park director showed up for our practice. Why shouldn't he attend practice? After all, we were the best team in the league. It turns out I should have been concerned. The park director had come to practice to evaluate me. He wanted to know if I was a liability to the park. After watching me play, he was afraid I would get hurt and the parks department would get sued. The park director called my father with the bad news. My father shared the bad news with me. My dreams, and my self-esteem, were shattered.

Many things have changed since 1963. We've sent men to stand on the moon. Computers fit in our laps. Small pox and polio have been driven from our shores. But one thing has not changed—it was just as difficult to find volunteers. So when Mrs. Alice Tewlewski stood up at the coach's meeting and said she wouldn't coach unless I, Tommy Rogers, was allowed to play on her team, the parks department had to rethink its decision.

After much discussion, the department decided I could play. It was a strange feeling to know I was suddenly deemed worthy. The park director hadn't reevaluated my skills. No, I was permitted to play because someone was willing to take a stand for *me*. Mrs. Tewlewski found something worthy in me, and she was willing to give up something if she couldn't have me on her team. She made me feel significant and useful. Mrs. Tewlewski demonstrated that I was a worthy person in her eyes.

If dear Mrs. Alice Tewlewski was able, through her offered sacrifice, to convince me that I had worth, imagine what the suffering and death of Jesus does to restore worth to the whole world. "God so loved [each of us] that He gave His one and only Son that whoever believes in Him shall not perish but have eternal life" (John 3:16). You are precious to God. He chose you for salvation and for His service before the very foundation of the world. People don't get any more special than you.

What a marvelous truth that is, but it's a truth that the devil fights against every day. And he fights hard. In fact, I think the devil succeeded for a time in convincing the apostle Paul of his unworthiness when Paul experienced his unknown "thorn in the flesh." Paul was so uncomfortable with it that he asked the Lord three times to remove it. Our Lord's response is good news to all who have "thorns," whether they're physical problems, emotional problems, or spiritual problems. Those things that cause us to limp through life are opportunities for God's strength to shine through our weakness.

Rather than hiding our faults from others, we can be who we are and know that God's power shines through our weaknesses. We don't need to be ashamed or afraid of our sins or our infirmities. God still uses us to accomplish His purposes. His power to turn defeats into victories is boldly demonstrated in Christ's resurrection. If God can bring joy and gladness out of death, He can bring hope and confidence to others through our shortcomings. Realizing God is at work in our lives makes us free to be who we are. God paid an incredible price for that freedom, it would be a shame to waste it.

I've witnessed the relationship between hundreds of church workers and the congregations they serve. Although I haven't visited every church in America, I believe I have visited enough to draw a few conclusions. Those congregations that have the hardest time affirming the leadership of professional church workers are those whose workers hide their vulnerability. The church workers continually blame their failures on others, trying valiantly to avoid being found deficient. Conversely, those churches who love their church workers generally are those whose workers easily confess and declare their weaknesses. These church workers aren't threatened by confession because they realize that those they serve soon learn about their deficiencies anyway. These church workers also know that God demonstrates His strength in their weaknesses.

Fellow church worker, you are a precious child of God. God called you to His service, not because you are without sin and difficulty, but because you are filled with sin and difficulty. God hires the handicapped and accomplishes in them more than anyone could ever imagine. His actions in your life bring Him glory.

You are God's favorite. God loves no one more than you, and He is proud of you. He is looking forward to spending eternity with you. Until that time, go ahead, limp. Let your weaknesses be seen because then God's people will love you all the more for your honesty and your courage. Such behavior makes God smile. And God will give you His comfort and fill you with His peace. Look for it in a package called self-esteem. Your self-esteem will not come from you, but it will, and does, come from Christ.

PRAYER

Heavenly Father, I believe You have an office, and on the walls of that office hang the pictures of each of Your children. You're proud of us because the lens you use to view us is the cross of Your Son, my Savior, Jesus. Help us to be proud in our weakness because of Your strength. In Jesus' name. Amen.

11

Till Death Us Do Part

I'm not sure why people choose to share their disappointment with church workers, but they do. And I'm definitely unclear about why they choose to share it as publicly as possible instead of in the privacy of an office. That happened to me today.

Last Sunday, I preached on the Epistle lesson, which was Hebrews 13:4, you know, "Marriage should be honored by all." I spoke of how the risen Christ empowers His people to keep the commitments and promises they make to each other, especially the commitment of marriage. I spoke of the witness young couples see when older couples celebrate their 40th, 50th, or 60th wedding anniversaries. I also mentioned that the same risen Christ has secured the forgiveness of sins for those who divorce. I tried to make it clear that God forgives because of the sacrifice of His Son, not because of the evil that existed in the marriage that some say made the divorce "necessary." This love, I said, sets us free to begin life again.

Apparently, one of our divorced members didn't hear a word of forgiveness. (I want to clarify that this isn't the first time I failed to make myself clear.) In Bible class, she asked why the only people who make good witnesses for the Lord are those who remain married. Couldn't divorced people also be good witnesses to the Lord? I quickly answered, "Absolutely! The blood of Jesus sets us free from all our sin." I shared again that if anyone is in Christ Jesus, they are a new creation, the old is gone away and behold the new has come. I shared that the church practices forgiveness as it welcomes divorced members to the Lord's Table, allows divorced members to teach Sunday school and Bible classes, and permits divorced members to serve as elders or even president of the congregation. All that is required is that the divorced member repents of their sins, and like all of us sinful and forgiven humans, promises to amend their sinful life.

That seemed to make this woman feel better, but it didn't do much for one of the visitors. As I spoke, his face contorted and he rolled his eyes. I could tell he didn't believe what he was hearing. I figured that he had probably experienced a difficult divorce and may be having a hard time understanding how his ex-wife could be forgiven. I decided to speak with the man after Bible class.

I welcomed the man, asked his name, and then expressed my concern about his uncomfortable looks during the class. He scoffed and told me that he was a fraternal life insurance salesman. But he hadn't always been an insurance salesman. For many years he had served as a pastor, but he and his wife divorced. The congregation he was serving decided it would be best if he left their service. He was wounded and hurt, so wounded that even though he was eligible for a call, he felt he couldn't, in good conscience, announce forgiveness to people who wouldn't forgive him. "Those things you told the woman about how the church welcomes a divorced person to teach Sunday school and Bible class, about how divorced people can serve as elders or even the president of the congregation, I just wish people would have been that generous to me," he said.

There wasn't a whole lot I could say in response. The man was right. Christians have trouble readily announcing to their professional church workers the forgiveness they freely grant one another. A more disturbing realization is that many of our faithful members have difficulty accepting that their church's professional leaders could have trouble in their relationships. Some members have even lost confidence in a leader because of a "chink" in the armor of the leader's family life.

In these tragic situations, the congregation and church worker often lose confidence in one another. Precisely when the church worker needs the congregation's support, the congregation might be the least willing to help. Instead, members opt to stand back and see how these men and women of God work out their problems by themselves, or with the help of the church's legal system or internal counseling system. Therefore, church workers experiencing family troubles, whether marital or child-related, often take their problems underground. They function as best they can from within a fog of anxiety that wears on them like a toothache.

Workers who trust the church body's internal counseling system might contact a circuit counselor or someone in the district office. But they often do so with a sense of panic. These circuit or district officials are the people who determine whether they can or should continue in the work they've been trained to do. Many church workers become reserved in the presence of their "superiors." Instead of spilling their guts and working toward a solution, church workers often just clear their throats and try not to shoot themselves in the foot.

What should be done with this unfortunate state of affairs? There's no simple answer, but I will suggest some possibilities for us to think about, pray about, and study.

First, it's almost a sure bet that the expectations of our congregation members aren't going to change. And that's not all bad. Professional church workers have been set apart since Pentecost because they are people of good character and "full of the Spirit and wisdom." Those chosen by Christ to enjoy the tremendous blessing of public service in the church need to feel set apart. We need to care about the stability of our families and marriages, not just for ourselves but for our Lord as well. But church workers can't take their families and family responsibilities lightly. It seems to me that we shouldn't decry the double standard that allows members to have family problems but not church workers.

Instead, we should celebrate the fact that God has chosen to place us under such an exacting standard.

Second, everyone, including the professional church worker, needs to understand that when we confess with the congregation that we are by nature sinful and unclean, we aren't lying. Despite our best intentions, despite our faithful use of Word and Sacrament, despite our prayers to the contrary, sometimes our commitments are broken. Marriages do break up. The belief that the church worker whose marriage ends in divorce is an aberration is an aberration to the church itself. It suggests that ordination, installation, or commissioning provides an inoculation to the evils that befall the rest of the world. The Scriptures are clear—we find our strength not in our work positions but in our Redeemer. When seen in the light of Christ's sacrifice, the gasps, the "oh nos," and the guffaws associated with church worker divorces should be replaced with understanding words such as "I need to call him" or "I'll bet this is a hard time for her" or "I just want you to know that we still love and support you."

Third, if strong relationships exist between colleagues and church officials are viewed as agents of care instead of agents of regulation, some professional tragedies could be avoided. Because we are sinful people, we often feel threatened by one another. Unfortunately, unhealthy competition between church workers with similar responsibilities and similar challenges can prevent them from befriending one another. Church officials, in an attempt to follow the "letter of the law," might miss opportunities to proclaim the Gospel to people who really need to hear it. When love—Christ's daring, selfless, even scandalous love—permeates our relationships, workers are strengthened and healed. As a result, losses to the church in terms of laborers in the vineyard will be diminished.

Fourth, fear needs to be driven from among us. "There is no fear in love. But perfect love drives out fear, because fear has to do with punishment. The one who fears is not made perfect in love" (1 John 4:18). Church workers who "walk on eggshells" during family troubles aren't as productive as they might otherwise be. Fear takes a lot of energy. Congregations that set aside the fear of criticism and don't constantly evaluate public opinion provide a bold witness to the Gospel of Christ, even if they have divorced church workers on their staff. The strength of our fellowship is in Jesus, not in the approval we receive from others.

Fifth, let's make it our business to bring our colleagues' marriages and families before our Lord in prayer. Our families and our marriages are some of the devil's favorite targets. We need to fight his fire with the fire from above, the Holy Spirit. Make time to share with one another the burdens of your heart. I don't appreciate it when people tell me how I should behave but then don't practice what they preach. So I'm going to make you a promise. If you are experiencing family or marital problems and you don't know where to turn, write or call me. You can contact me through Concordia Publishing House. I can't promise you solutions, but I can promise you willing ears and a heart that cares.

PRAYER

Lord, You made it clear that stoning someone takes a valuable resource from Your earthly kingdom. Help us drop our stones, turn away from our sins, and serve You enthusiastically. In Jesus' name. Amen.

12

TIME MANAGEMENT

I was in the hospital room of a friend and member who was about to undergo an angioplasty. His family members gathered around the bed. Although we knew this procedure is considered "safe," we couldn't help wondering whether everything would be all right. Given this emotionally charged atmosphere, you would expect some important, significant things to be said. That's why I was surprised when, after hearing that the doctors performing the procedure set their own schedule, my friend said, "In that regard, they are a lot like preachers." Putting his hand on my shoulder, he announced to his family that he had been trying to get me on a schedule for years.

Although literally facing a life-or-death procedure (he's now healthier than ever), this man used precious time to talk to me about time management. Such significant words indicate how important our time-management decisions are, not only to us but to our members as well.

The business community has provided the church with many time-management models. As prolific as these plans and models are, one consistent theme runs through them all—to make wise use of your time on a consistent basis, you must adopt a regular schedule.

Studying how we schedule our time immediately identifies our priorities. For example, people in the business community schedule their lives around work (or acquiring money, which isn't wrong as long as it's kept in perspective) and their families. Those who are dedicated to playing sports—golfers, tennis players, fishermen, and the like—organize their schedules around tee times, tennis matches, or fishing trips. Others focus their schedules on watching sports. They pay attention to the date and time of the next college or professional baseball, football, or basketball game. Grandparents schedule opportunities to spend time with their grandchildren. Gym rats, a generally ambitious segment of society, organize their time around their next work out. The less ambitious among us schedule time around the sofa and the next commercial. In summary, we schedule our time around what is important to us.

Jesus was no different. We can learn a lot about time management from His example. Jesus organized His life around service to His Father and the people His Father loves. From His youth, Jesus' schedule centered around His Father's will. Even though Mary and Joseph didn't understand or appreciate the three extra days Jesus spent at the temple, He remained because He had to be about His "Father's business."

When Mary and Martha summoned Jesus to the death bed of Lazarus, their brother and Jesus' friend, it took Him four days to arrive. By then Lazarus was dead. Mary expressed their grief and disappointment, "Lord, if You had been here, my brother would not have died." Essentially, Mary was telling Jesus she didn't think He'd made the most of His time.

Between Jesus' resurrection and His ascension, His disciples asked, "Lord, are You at this time going to restore the kingdom to Israel?" Some still believed Jesus hadn't managed His time well because they hoped His time was organized around political concerns. Instead, Jesus focused His time-management skills on fulfilling His Father's mission, namely the salvation of the world from sin, death, and the power of the devil. Any time-management principle employed by a church worker needs to be rooted and grounded in that same mission to proclaim Christ's life-changing Gospel.

Many adhere to the principle that a happy church worker is a healthy church worker. These individuals make sure to spend time exercising. While it's indeed God-pleasing to care for our bodies, what happens if someone stops you on the way to the gym, just to talk? Do you make time in your schedule to meet with this person who might be confused, burdened, bothered, or upset? It's our responsibility to wrap our time around those people who need Christ's love.

Church workers need to spend time with their families. Time together eases the stresses and stains of both the church worker and the family. Vacations provide church workers and their families opportunity for renewal and restoration. Unlike other employees, we don't work 50 weeks a year to get our two weeks of vacation. We work to praise our Savior and to demonstrate His love to the world. What more powerful demonstration of His love than to organize our vacations around the needs of those we serve? We may even, on occasion, need to change or cut short our plans if the people we serve require it.

The importance of continuing education for professional church workers cannot be underestimated. But continuing education takes time. Hopefully, the congregation will happily allow a church worker to take time for continuing education, if you work around the congregation's schedule and needs. By being considerate of your congregation's claims on your time, you demonstrate Christ's love, and your own, to the people you serve.

I'm not suggesting that time management that revolves around proclaiming the Gospel is easy. In fact, I believe that it's more difficult to learn and put into practice than a time-management system that follows step-by-step directions. A Gospel-driven time-management system originates in the heart, not in the head. This system doesn't center around a principle but around a person—Jesus Christ, the Savior and servant of the world, who calls us to take up our cross and follow Him.

Our church has a Saturday worship service at 5 p.m. One Saturday, at about 3:30 p.m., my home phone rang. A new member wanted to tell me her daughter had just given birth to a little girl who wasn't expected to live. She wanted someone to come and baptize her grandchild. Because the hospital was 20 miles away by interstate, I knew I could never get there, baptize the baby, and get back for the evening service. I tried calling one of our other pastors, but no one was home. I could have asked an elder to baptize the baby (it was an emergency), but I decided to go myself. I would just make the best time I could.

I left a message on the answering machine at church, warning the elder assigned for that service, and rushed to the hospital. I prayed with the family, baptized the baby, prayed with the family again, jumped in the car, and headed to church. May God forgive me for the way I drove, but I pulled into the parking lot at exactly 5:30. The head elder was pacing outside the church. "Lou, did you get my message about what's going on?" I asked. "No, Pastor, but you can explain to me and the congregation at the same time. They're waiting for you," he replied.

I walked into the sanctuary and was confronted by a sea of faces, all looking at me. Some faces showed concern. Some registered amusement. Some people looked angry. I stood in the center aisle and said, "Folks, let me tell you what I've been doing." I reached into my pocket and pulled out the vial I had been given in the hospital. It had held the water I used to baptize the baby. I held it up for everyone to see and said, "This is what I've been up to." I explained about the baby and her severe illness at birth. I told them that God had given us the gift of

Baptism so that all nations, including sick little babies and their distraught parents, could know that they are heirs of heaven because of what Jesus did for them on the cross. I told them that we, as a congregation, had given that family a tremendous gift—the peace that passes all understanding. Because of this means of grace, if anything does happen to that baby, the parents know that she will spend forever in the arms of her Savior.

Now, there were many different kinds of people in the congregation that night. Some worshipers were new to Christianity and weren't really sure what Baptism really meant. Some people had lost children and knew exactly what comfort Baptism brought. Others in the congregation were extremely "organized" people who expect that the pastor will be at church at least one hour before the worship service begins. But they all rejoiced that death once again had been mocked by God's means of grace.

We celebrated the Lord's Supper that night. It seemed an especially wonderful celebration that evening. We had been reminded that we—church worker, congregation, and a sick little girl—are the center of God's schedule. He has planned all His days, even eternity, around us. Before the service ended, word came that the little girl had gone to heaven. Once again the Lord reminded us not just to number our days but even to number our minutes.

One member in attendance that evening is a university professor and a former director of Christian education. A week or so after the service, he spoke to me about his thoughts as he sat waiting for me to arrive. He explained that his stomach was in knots as he heard me explain my late arrival. He recalled his own days in parish ministry and confessed that he was absolutely sure he wouldn't have gone to the hospital. He said his actions would have been motivated by fear of how the congregation would have reacted.

Our Lord doesn't want us to be motivated by fear. He wants our motivation to be love. That's what He has freed us for—to spend our days freely and courageously serving Him. That may mean we spend five hours one week preparing for our sermon or Bible study or youth group meeting and only 50 minutes the next because a family or committee or young person needed the other four hours. That's okay. In fact, it's more than okay, it's divine, or rather it models the divine—Jesus Himself.

Jesus based His comings and goings on people's needs. His birth, which occurred at the "fullness of time," not in "split-second timing," was for the sake of people. He waited 30 years to begin His public ministry, a ministry that brought sight to the blind, hope to the hopeless, life to those who had died. Jesus' ministry took place in God's time, for the sake of His people.

Know that your time, too, is guided, directed, and organized by your Lord Jesus. Take time for exercise, rest, study, and family, but organize your time around people and their need for Jesus. You won't just be organizing time, you'll be serving eternity.

PRAYER

Lord, help us understand that time is Your gift to us. Help us use it as You used Your time, placing people's need for a Savior first. In Jesus' name. Amen.

13

THE BLESSING OF MINISTRY

I wake up every morning and give thanks to God for the work He's called me to do. Some mornings I say the prayer loudly. Today, I prayed it quietly. Some members of our Christ-serving staff disagreed on how to handle a situation. Because I'm the "senior pastor," it's my job to help them resolve the problem. We talked and talked and talked. This particular discussion was in addition to the numerous times we've talked and talked and talked about the issue. We talk, but no one wants to compromise. I know that when this issue is finally resolved, someone will be called right and someone will be called wrong. The person identified as wrong will probably be me. Senior pastor, teacher, youth worker, janitor, teacher's aide—we all can find ourselves in corners from which we can't extricate ourselves. We pray, trust, and do what we think is best for the church. Yes, there's always criticism. Yes, the frustration level rises. But Jesus is still Lord of the church.

After that emotional meeting, one person left smiling, the other left crying, and I caught my breath and took my blood pressure medicine. Then I went to check the mail. Our treasurer stopped me to inform me that the offering was down last week, just like the previous week. "We're gonna have to do something about that," he said. While that's what he said, he meant to say that *I* should do something about the offerings. I know; I will. Lord show me what to do.

Last week I spoke to a parenting group at a sister congregation. I spent a lot of time preparing. I delivered my material with a special passion. I was using the best of my God-given abilities to help those families in their relationships with one another and with Christ. I went home with the thank-yous of many people ringing in my ears.

Although the sounds of praise were fading, I could still hear them two days later when I opened a note from someone who had been in attendance. He wrote, "Last evening in your talk delivered at our church, you used the word *nuclear*." He was right, I had. I used the word while discussing how parents talk to their teenagers, especially how parents should use the word *no*. I told the group not to use *no* unless it was absolutely necessary. "Instead, try to talk things out with your kids," I explained. "Help them arrive at their own no. The minute we say 'no,' it's like we've launched a nuclear weapon." Remember, I was really committed to what I was saying. When that happens, I don't always speak the king's English. I'm more interested in announcing our King of king's reign and rule. As a result of my enthusiasm, I apparently mispronounced the word as *nukclur* (according to this person). He didn't like my misuse of the language. He thought I could do better. That's all he had to say about my presentation. It wasn't a great day.

As I worked in my backyard that evening, I wondered why I hadn't taken over my dad's plumbing business. I prayed a little and then complained to the Lord a little. "Why do I have to put up with all these petty things?" I asked. "I've read the book of Acts several times. Those folks didn't seem to have all this trouble. They seemed to go from one victory to another."

I was wide awake, but as I continued to talk and pray, I began to daydream about my early days in the ministry. I remembered hugging new fathers outside delivery rooms. I remembered applauding for a young man on the football field. He'd been horrible in confirmation class, but at that moment he was focused, a contributor, dare I even say, a leader?

Then I recalled a 12-year-old blond kid I had known while I was in New Orleans. His parents had just joined our church. Even though I had never met this boy, I'd heard about him. "He's a troublemaker. Keep him away from your daughters," I was told. He didn't look menacing to me, but looks can be deceiving. When confirmation class started, I quickly discovered that this boy, Cody, wasn't interested in anything I tried to teach him. He disrupted the class in every way possible. Cody spent more time outside the classroom door than he did inside the room. Well, that's not entirely true. Cody wouldn't stay outside the door for long. He'd wander off to entertain himself, someplace away from my supervision. Other staff members and I met with Cody on weekends and after school to finish his confirmation preparation.

With a lot of hard work and help from his parents, Cody was ready to be confirmed with the rest of his class. On that special day, he was his extraordinary self. Cody wore his corsage upside down, and his white gown was adjusted to sag and slump in all the "hip" places. After his confirmation, we rarely saw Cody. He stopped attending church. He sometimes came to youth group but only for a short time, and his presence was always disruptive. Cody wasn't a "good" kid. For some reason, I loved him and so did his family, which couldn't have been easy.

Cody's dad would talk to me occasionally about the difficulties they were having with him. It seemed Cody would wait until his family was asleep and then sneak out his window and head for any place where he could get into trouble. Because his family lived in New Orleans, he usually headed for the French Quarter. Cody knew it like the back of his hand. His parents usually caught him trying to sneak back into the house. They tried to impress on him the danger of such activity, not to mention how unhealthy it was to go without adequate sleep. Their words fell on deaf ears.

The family discussions grew into arguments, which grew in intensity and even bordered on violence. Cody's parents decided to seek professional help. To make sure no stone was left unturned, they asked me if I would visit Cody. Every Tuesday afternoon I picked Cody up at his house and took him to a local restaurant. I bought him a soda and some french fries. He would eat, and I would talk. In fact all he would do was eat. I hoped he was listening as I told him that he couldn't continue to alienate his parents, his teachers, even the police. I knew he wasn't listening. After a few months, Cody said, "P.T., I'm just the way I am. God made me this way, and I can't change. Everyone has to make a decision—do you want me in your life or don't you? It doesn't matter to me. Just know that I'm not changing for anybody."

The next week, Cody ran away. For months no one knew where he was, and we feared the worst. Just when I had given up hope, Cody's father came to church to speak with me. "Pastor, Cody's in trouble. He sold drugs to some people. When they didn't pay him, Cody got a gun and tried to shoot them. Thankfully, he missed, but he was arrested."

Cody's dad asked me to visit the boy in jail. I did. It broke my heart. There was this blond-headed boy, no longer in a confirmation robe but in an inmate uniform in the Orleans Parish Prison. "Cody, I really want to help you. Everyone wants to help you. Just let us," I said. "Can you get me out of here, P.T.?" he asked. "No, Cody, I can't get you out," I answered. "Then we have nothing to talk about," Cody replied. I don't think I accomplished much with Cody while he was in jail. But I did bring him markers. Cody was an artist—a clever artist. He flaired the felt strip inside the marker before inserting it back into the marker's tube. Thus, he created a paint brush.

Each time I visited, Cody showed me his latest creations. They were magnificent but depressing. All Cody's artwork followed the same theme—figures of suffering, tortured humans against a background of eerie demons. Figures that resembled survivors emerging from World War II concentration camps were everywhere in his pictures. In the right corner of every one of Cody's drawings was a goat's head, a symbol for Satan. The first time I saw one of these works, I asked Cody, "Where do you get this stuff?" He answered without missing a beat and without any apology, "P.T., this is what I see when I do LSD. And P.T., I do a lot of LSD." Cody's frankness frightened me. I told him I'd try to help him if ever he wanted to leave the drug lifestyle behind. It's all I could say. He grunted, "Yeah, sure," and that was the end of the conversation.

I was ineffective in my ministry with Cody, but God was working overtime. He put Cody before a judge who decided it would be healthier for Cody to spend time in drug rehabilitation rather than in jail. I drove Cody home from court that day. He wasn't happy. He thought about running away but opted against it. The center was in a distant state, and Cody thought it might be a challenge. We thought it might give him a fresh start. We were sure that Cody was going to a place that would make a difference.

Maybe that's why his family and I were so disappointed several months later when we heard the disturbing news. Cody had broken some of the center's covenants and agreements and had been asked to leave. He was returned to New Orleans and placed in a psychiatric hospital a few miles from his home and the church. Old friends from his rebellious days, family members, youth group members, and I immediately began visiting Cody. While the "old friends" dropped off the list, his parents, brothers, youth group members, and I continued to see him.

Cody continued to draw and paint while in the hospital. The hideous artwork made my skin crawl, but I kept asking to see each new piece. And with each new piece, I made the same request, "Cody, if you ever want to change, to make a new start, let me know. Call me anytime."

One day, Cody called me from his hospital room. He called at 2 a.m. I was so excited. I called the hospital and explained to the operator that Cody had just called and that I needed to see him immediately. I asked which door I should use to enter. The operator asked if I was aware that it was 2 a.m. When I assured her that I knew what time it was, she proceeded to say, "Reverend, if you think you can get into a psychiatric hospital at 2 a.m., you are absolutely crazy." I promised her that I could provide proof of that fact within 30 minutes if she would give me the opportunity. She wouldn't. With the help of a psychologist friend who practiced at that facility, I finally got inside. I couldn't help but think of the people who've called me "nuts" as we stealthily moved from staircase to elevator, past the nurses' station, and into Cody's room. If I'm so "nuts," I wondered, why am I having so much trouble getting into this place?

Cody's room was pitch black as I entered. His cigarette glowed in the darkness. "P.T., I'm impressed. I didn't think you'd be able to make it," Cody said. I wasn't amused. In my most pastoral voice, I said, "Cody, this better be important because if it isn't, I'm going to kill you!"

"It's important, P.T.," Cody said. He told me that he knew if he kept heading in the same direction, he was going to die. He wasn't ready to die. He admitted that he was in trouble, big trouble, and that if he was going to be "saved" from the mess he'd created, his help would have to come from God. I assured him that God would be quick to save. Cody said that I didn't know the whole story. When he was running with the drug-selling crowd, he used to hang around with people who wore "funny robes, used funny prayer books, brought blood and animals, and talked a lot about serving Satan.

"I was there, P.T.," he said. "I watched the whole thing, and I didn't care. I didn't care what they did. P.T., after all I've done, I can't believe that God would still want to help me."

I knew that God had brought us to a crossroads—literally the "cross" road. I asked God to give me the words to say that would set Cody free. "Cody, do you know that before the world began, God knew that you and I would be here this evening? Before the world began, God knew that He would create us and that we would fall from His grace. God knew that our sin would put our lives in great peril, that we would die eternally because of our sin. That's why He sent Jesus to suffer and die for our sins. That's why Jesus gave us the gift of Baptism.

"Baptism is God's way of letting you and me know that what Jesus accomplished on the cross was accomplished for us. Baptism is God's way of claiming us forever. On the day of our Baptism, God declares to the devil that this person is Mine and will be forever. That's what happened at your Baptism, Cody. God claimed you as His child forever. Right now, as you and I speak, God is mocking the devil. He's telling the devil that even though Satan thought he had you, God trumped him with the saving love poured out on you at your Baptism. You are a child of God, Cody. That will never change, no matter what you've done. For Jesus' sake, you are forgiven."

Together, in the darkness, we confessed our sins. We heard the Good News of forgiveness. We gave thanks. We embraced. When it was daylight and legal, I returned to Cody's room to celebrate Holy Communion. I believe it was the first time Cody had taken the Sacrament since his confirmation. As I prepared, I put out two hosts and two cups of wine. I told Cody that we would take Communion together. At the appropriate time, I would give him the body and blood of Christ, then he would give me the body and blood of Christ. He paused and asked if that was permissible. He was afraid he wasn't worthy. What a wonderful opportunity God provided to share again with Cody the completeness of Christ's forgiveness. "Cody, when you go home, your mother's going to make you set the table, clean up after meals, and maybe even make you cook. When you're at home as a family member, Cody, you get to serve at the table. Cody, you're home. You get to serve at the table." We shared the Lord's Supper together.

Cody was a new man. He started to get along with his family. He made plans to return to school. He was released from the hospital. He even came back to church. The whole congregation rejoiced.

After services one Sunday, Cody asked me to stop by his house that week. The agreed upon day turned out to be damp and rainy. I didn't want to go, but I had promised. Upon arriving, I discovered the purpose of the meeting was to reveal the latest drawing. As I looked at it, I panicked. The same demons served as the background. The central image was that of a young man with horns on his head and his head in his hands. Cody later described my reaction as "going ballistic."

"P.T., chill out," Cody said. "What is the dude sitting on in the picture?" I responded that it looked like a large hand. Cody said I was right and then asked me who else was in the picture. "Jesus, and He's suffering on the cross," I answered, referring to another prominent image. Cody again confirmed my answer. "P.T., do you see another hand?" he asked. I pointed to one coming down from the top of the page. "This hand is coming down from on high. And it's holding Jesus' hand while He hangs on the cross. And if you look closely, P.T., the hand holding the suffering guy is connected to the hand Jesus is holding.

"They are the hands of God," Cody explained. "And, P.T., the suffering guy is me. God is holding both His boys in His hands, Jesus and me. Jesus is suffering for my sins, and I'm suffering because of them. All this suffering takes place in the face of the demons. Through Jesus' suffering, God is giving life to us both, right in the presence of the demons and the devil. And

101

there's nothing they can do about it. P.T., I know whose I am."

The angels in heaven couldn't have been rejoicing more than I was. I left Cody's house walking two feet above the ground. I thought, my boy is home free!

I have never been prophetic before and I hope to never be prophetic again. Two nights later, I got a call from Methodist Hospital. My friend Cody had been shot by one of his drug "friends." I got there as quickly as I could, but it was too late. Cody was already gone. As I walked away from the blood-filled emergency room, I was tempted to think that we had lost and the devil had won. All of us—parents, brothers, family members, church members, pastors—we had lost. Cody was dead.

Then I remembered the drawing. I remembered the hands of God that held Jesus and gave Him life and held Cody and had given him life. I had told Cody that what he had been drawing were images of conflict, conflict that had been conquered by Christ. I told him that one book of the Bible was a book of conflict. God gave it to His people to let us know that no matter how hard life might be, God will give us the victory.

I took Cody through the Revelation of St. John. He particularly appreciated the vision in the first chapter where Jesus is described in all His splendor. I asked Cody to draw that vision and then we would work together to explain what the picture meant. That way, we would help others understand God's victory as described in Revelations. Cody was excited about the venture. Now the throne room of God was open to Cody, and he saw His God face to face. Regardless of how hard the devil had tried to claim Cody, he had failed. Christ had conquered. My man was home free.

On the day of his funeral, Cody's mother shared something with me. It was the last thing she found on his drawing board—a charcoal sketch of Revelation 1. Cody had begun to try to interpret for others the glory of God. What he hadn't accomplished on paper, he had accomplished in life. He had allowed us to see Jesus transform a rebellious young sinner into a faithful servant.

I shared Cody's story with the hundreds who attended his funeral—young and old. As I walked away from his grave, I found myself chanting some familiar words. I would like to tell you that they were the words of a powerful Bible passage. I would like to tell you they were the words of a great Easter hymn. But they weren't. They were words that I had heard a million times in the New Orleans Superdome when it looked like the Saints were going to defeat their opponent. In true New Orleans' style, the fans would chant, "Who dat? Who dat? Who dat say dey gonna beat dem Saints!" Feeling guilty about focusing on such a trite statement, I changed it a bit. Somehow it sounds better as "Who dat? Who dat? Who dat say dey gonna beat *God's* saints!"

Jesus had reached down and grabbed Cody eternally in his Baptism. Just when the devil was reaching out in that emergency room to grab Cody for himself, Jesus put His nail-scarred hands on my friend, sheltered him in His arms, and chanted at the prince of demons, "Who dat? Who dat? Who dat say dey gonna beat God's saints!"

Brothers and sisters, that's our mission and ministry in a nutshell. In a world filled with temptations and the fruit of sin—pain, fear, anger, and death—you and I have been given the privilege of standing up to the evil one. We proclaim every day, in the strong name of Jesus and with all the power of the resurrection, "Who dat? Who dat? Who dat say dey gonna beat God's saints!"

Brothers and sisters in Christ's service, that's our calling, our mission, to boldly proclaim every day, even in the face of the demons and the prince of darkness, "Who do you think you are?" I invite you to get used to the phrase, commit it to memory, use it against the evil one. Say it with me, "Who dat? Who dat? Who dat say dey gonna beat God's saints!"

Our ministry does not call us to resolve squabbles, endure criticism, handle financial crises, or make neurotic people feel happy and safe. Our ministry calls us to handle all these situations and more with the words, "Who dat? Who dat? Who dat say dey gonna beat God's saints!" What a sublime calling. What a courageous vocation. What a blessing it is to realize that God uses us to put the devil on notice that he is defeated eternally.

That calling is yours. Go into the world in peace. Have courage. Hold on to what is good. Don't return evil for evil. Restore the fainthearted. Honor all people. Love and serve the Lord, rejoicing in the power of the Holy Spirit. Listen to the complainers and love them. Handle the financial problems with courage. Care for the sick. Direct the confused. Love the loveless. And do it in such a way that the devil, the world, and our flesh knows that no one can beat God's saints! And may God the Father, God the Son, and God the Holy Spirit bless you!

PRAYER

Father, we thank You for the work You have entrusted into our care. Angels are envious of our work. Help us remember the triumphs You have graciously allowed us to know and help us share the joy Your Son won for us. In Jesus' name. Amen.

14

NETWORKING

The 1990s were not necessarily good years for Californians. Riots, earthquakes, fires, and the O. J. Simpson "trial of the century" generated a lot of press. For those of us who love the state, we've hated to see the negative impressions these events have caused. These incidents have caused tremendous heartache and contributed to a sagging economy. In the 1980s, California's economy was fueled by the defense industry. Recent downsizing caused by the dissolution of the Soviet Union has affected every social and business structure in the state, even the church.

As a congregation, we have watched men and women who have served responsibly for years in their workplace lose their jobs. And they're losing good jobs. Thousands of skilled professionals who've never had to look for a job suddenly find themselves struggling to find employment. As I helped these men and women, one word came up again and again—networking. People told me they were establishing a network, which they believed would be the key to finding a job. As our unemployed workers found new positions, I discovered they were absolutely right. Those who had established good networks got jobs. Those who hadn't established networks remained unemployed for longer periods of time.

I believe many people would agree that networking proves the truth of the saying, "It's not *what* you know, it's *who* you know." But after what I've seen, I would have to disagree. I believe it's more accurate to say, "It's not who you *know,* it's who you *are.*"

I didn't reach this conclusion by observing the secular world. I reached it by observing the church. I once had the opportunity to mentor a young man who was preparing for the pastoral ministry. I looked forward to providing direction and offering him the benefit of my experience. But he made it clear that he didn't need my help. After all, he had "been around," and he had "paid attention." He proclaimed that he was already as good as two-thirds of the pastors he had met and he hadn't even finished the seminary. Arrogance is a hard thing for a pastor to fit under his vestments. And this guy's alb was stuffed.

When it came time for this young man to enter the public ministry, much to my surprise those considering calling him for service called to talk to me. No one asked about his academic background. No one inquired whether he showed up for work on time. No one even asked about his ability as a preacher or his administrative skills. The first question out of everyone's mouth was, "Is he a good guy?" As I tried to come up with an honest answer that still met Luther's enjoinder in the explanation to the Eighth Commandment to "put the best construction on everything," a light went on. I thought, we're networking. The church is networking!

We certainly do network, and it's not a new occurrence. It goes all the way back to the book of Acts when the early church's leaders were trying to select faithful people to accomplish certain tasks. People were needed to take over waiting on tables so the apostles could carry out, without distraction, their God-given assignment to preach the Gospel. The criteria for serving as waiters was simple: The candidates must have been "known to be full of the Spirit and wisdom." In modern terms, I think that means they were "good guys."

What determines whether a church worker is a "good guy" or a "good gal"? The best answer might be to quote the Supreme Court justice who was asked to define pornography. He said, "I can't define it, but I know it when I see it." In the church, there isn't a report card we're measured against. But some characteristics certainly tip us off that someone is "good."

Humility is important. In 1986, Pope John Paul II visited the United States. His itinerary included a stop in New Orleans. The Pope stayed at Notre Dame Seminary during his New Orleans visit. He attended morning Mass, which is his daily habit. When he entered the chapel, the Pope saw that he was the only person in attendance, and he had arrived a little late. The young priest officiating didn't notice the grey-haired man, clad in T-shirt and jeans, enter the room. Only when this casually dressed man came up and held his service book open for him did the priest realize anyone was present. To the young priest's amazement, his altar boy was the Pope. Good guys and gals are humble, easy to be around, and always more ready to serve than to be served.

A sense of humor, even self-directed humor, is important. A preacher who is bold enough to suggest that last Sunday he had a dream he was preaching, and woke up to discover that he was, is a delight to be around. A person whose laugh is deep, frequent, and sincere makes every situation, even difficult ones, more bearable.

Generosity is a key attribute. It's hard to get close to someone who's always carefully counting and comparing the hours each of you work, the compliments each of you receive, or the change you each get from the waitress after your bill is paid. It isn't earth-shattering, but it's easier to relax and feel refreshed when the person you eat lunch with is more concerned with your fellowship than with being "stuck" for an unfair amount of the check.

Good people listen to your ideas. They respect and value your opinions because they respect and value you. Your value doesn't depend on your intelligence or wit. Rather you are valued because you are fearfully and wondrously made! You are God's child. God has something special going on in your life and good people recognize that.

Good people keep their mouths shut. When you speak privately to a good guy or gal, your words, thoughts, and feelings are kept in confidence. You don't have to worry about someone violating your trust to prove that they are privy to special information.

You can depend on good people. One of my closest friends is someone who encapsulates all these qualities, but perhaps his greatest attribute is his dependability. Most people don't like visiting the hospital. Such trips usually aren't enjoyable. When we do go, we generally stay for a respectable amount of time and move on. Few of us would consider making the effort to get into the surgery waiting room for anyone except a family member. Recently, my family couldn't be with me as I waited for a surgical procedure. But my friend was. Pastors spend a great deal of time praying with and holding the hands of people who are awaiting surgery. Sometimes we wonder who will pray with us or hold our hands as we face surgery. Now I know who would be with me—my good friend Jack.

A good person is someone you are proud to introduce as a friend. And that's what networking is—friends proudly introducing one another to the church and world. Networking is selflessly sharing gifts and skills with others so that together we can accomplish more than any of us could alone.

Good people practice daily repentance and forgiveness. "I'm sorry" comes easily to their lips and with similar ease and conviction, "Please forgive me" is uttered when appropriate and necessary. Good people do not stand on pride or office.

In short, the presence of a good person is a blessing to you. You proudly introduce this person to others as your friend and coworker.

Jesus knew all about networking. He describes it in John 17. In verse 1, Jesus says, "Father, the time has come. Glorify Your Son, that Your Son may glorify You." Now that's networking. That's appreciating each other so much that you share each other's strengths and abilities with the world. In verse 6, Jesus says, "[Father,] I have revealed You to those whom You gave me out of the world." Jesus spent three years introducing His disciples to His Father. He wanted them to know about God's love and faithfulness. He wanted to demonstrate to them God's power and might. Jesus repeatedly emphasized the wonderful attributes of His Father. He said that God had made and would continue to make a blessed difference in the disciples' lives. That's networking.

In verse 8, Jesus continues, "I gave them the words You gave Me and they accepted them. They knew with certainty that I came from You." The network was complete. Jesus was connected with His Father, and His Father, because of Jesus, was connected with the disciples. The power of God's Holy Spirit working through that network can be found throughout the book of Acts. The Gospel goes from Jerusalem to Judea, to Samaria, to the ends of the earth.

And the network keeps growing. In verse 20, Jesus says that He doesn't just pray for the 12 disciples, but He prays for those who will believe in Him because of the disciples' testimony. Jesus is praying for you and me. By the power of the Holy Spirit, we believe the disciples' testimony and we thank God for those who gave it to us.

As Jesus prays for you and me in verse 20, He prays that we may be one, just as He and the Father are one. Our Lord Jesus longs for the day when all His people are networked. Our ability to network can impact the salvation of the world. We have a tremendous responsibility to network as magnificently as possible, to embrace others who serve with us in the vineyard.

But sin gets in the way of our ability to network effectively. Sin causes us to pass judgment on one another. Sin causes us to place ourselves in higher positions than the Scriptures say we should take. But Jesus has given us the victory over sin, death, and the power of the devil. We can look at one another through the eyes of Christ and declare that we are working with good people.

Jesus enables us to see past the faults of our friends and coworkers and celebrate the gifts they have been given. Jesus enables us to forgive the sins of our brothers and sisters. He enables us to embrace their humility, rejoice in their sense of humor, celebrate their generosity. He enables us to thank God for their ability to listen, to be grateful for their ability to maintain confidences, to depend on their dependability, and to be proud to introduce them to our friends.

In recent years, I have been privileged to travel around the country speaking at church-related workshops and conferences. I am impressed at the great work God is doing in all of us. I would be proud to introduce most of the church workers I have met as my friends. They have obviously been networked with Christ.

Let's see to it that each of us prays for the power to expand our network. Our churches have been blessed by that network for decades; it is at the heart of our system for preparing professional church workers and calling them to ministry. So let the network grow. Let it grow in love, in mutual appreciation, in respect, and in forgiveness. May we all know the joy that comes to those who are spoken well of by their peers. May we all know the joy of networking in Christ's church.

PRAYER

Father, thanks for our salvation. Now help us live lives characterized by humility, a sense of humor, generosity, listening skills, confidentiality, and reliability so that we might bring glory to You as we are called "good guys" and "good gals." In Jesus' name. Amen.

15

GOD NEEDS YOU ... NOW

The lights of a truck approached. I assumed it carried yet another lifeguard who wanted to question us. I was wrong. Instead, it held a silent lifeguard, an individual as quiet as the parents of my best friend. They sat, grim-faced, beside him on the front seat. Steve, their son, had joined my church youth group for a beach party. We had spent a glorious day in the California sun and water. Suddenly, the fun was over; the day turned dark. We had gotten out of the water to dry off and play some volleyball. As we divided into teams, we noticed that Steve was missing. The last time anyone saw him was in the water.

We ran to the lifeguard station. The lifeguards spent an hour searching. Then they shoved a boat into the water, pulling a dragnet to search the bottom of the ocean for the body of my friend.

As we watched the hideous sight, the senior lifeguard approached me and said it was time to call Steve's family. I remember thinking how glad I was that it wasn't my job to tell the bad news. The lifeguard called the police department in our hometown. The police sent officers to Steve's house to tell his parents that their son had drowned. But the police officers didn't share the bad news. They simply said to call the lifeguard station. And the lifeguards didn't share the bad news either. They told Steve's parents to come to the beach. When his frantic parents finally arrived where our group was gathered, they still hadn't heard the bad news.

I'll never forget the empty feeling that washed over me as Steve's mom looked at me and asked, "Tommy, what on earth is wrong with Steve?" I realized that his parents knew nothing about what had happened. I hugged Steve's mother and whispered, "I'm so sorry. They think Steve drowned." We spent the rest of the night holding one another's hands, combing the dark beach, hoping against hope to find Steve. His parents prayed he was playing some sick practical joke. His body was found several days later, two weeks before our high school graduation.

My 17-year-old mind and heart couldn't forgive the police or the lifeguards for the horrible position they put me in that night. In fact, it took several years before I fully understood what had taken place that night. I learned that being a public servant does not automatically enable you to bring devastating information to unsuspecting people. But God makes sure people are present to get the job done. And God doesn't care if that person is 17 or 71.

When God gives someone a gift or ability, He calls that person to service, sometimes without warning or practice. God places the mantle of ministry on your shoulders and empowers you to serve. God bestows the ultimate compliment on His children when He chooses them to bring love and hope into what otherwise might be considered a hopeless situation. God has placed His hand on you too. You perform a job no one else can do, at the very time and place God wants you to be doing it.

Certainly we're not called to be the bearers of bad news, but God makes sure we're in the right situation at the right time. What about the well-meaning but unintentionally divisive person who disrupts congregation meetings with critical or negative remarks? You may be the only person that individual will listen to. I think I can say, without exaggeration, that God has used you to avoid a division in your church. And what about the secretary who seems to rub everyone the wrong way? Staff members clamor for dismissal. You know that dismissal would cause chaos in the secretary's family. God uses you as a peacemaker, a go-between to smooth the situation between the secretary and those who would rather be "piece" makers. If you weren't around, feelings could be hurt for years.

There will be times when you wish you weren't so gifted. Why can't someone else play the organ for this record-setting Easter crowd? Why do I have to watch my hair turn gray as I spend long weekends with the irascible children of nonsupportive parents? Simply put, the answer to these questions is because the Almighty needs you at the organ, at the lock-in, at the sick-bed, at the church office, at the congregation meeting.

I still hear from Steve's parents. Interestingly, our encounters come whenever I begin questioning my competence as a minister. Twenty-five years after that tragedy, those people still remember the hugs, the tears, the love, and the care they received from someone who hadn't attended the seminary or college, from someone who hadn't even graduated from high school. The only credential I possessed was the love of God. But those dear people believe they were blessed by my presence.

The real blessing was mine. Through Steve's death, God granted me wisdom for life. Let me explain. Steve and I spent high school planning for the future. Because neither of us was particularly gifted with looks, intelligence, athletic ability, or popularity, we were committed to rectifying that situation. We planned to study hard, save money, and enter a good university. Then we would make something of ourselves. Because we were living for the future, we passed up many opportunities to do things in the present, such as ball games, dances, and parties, so we could study. We believed we were doing what was best for our future.

Tragically, only one of us had a future, and the one with the future was no longer sure how to live in a world that seemed futureless. I was confused until I remembered the gift—the call to ministry, God's gift that allowed me to love and comfort someone in the name of Jesus. This wonderful call to ministry assures us that even if we have a brief future or no future according to earthly standards, our lives have eternal meaning and purpose. God has used us to spread the message of His salvation.

Six of us served as Steve's pallbearers. As we left the grave site, one pallbearer exclaimed, "What a waste." For a long time, every visit I made to Steve's grave seemed to underscore the truth of those words. I still visit Steve's grave about four times a year. I go, not as a grieving teenager, but as a pastor who has the privilege of proclaiming the powerful name of the Lord of life in this place of the dead. God didn't waste this tragedy. He used it to call someone into a special work that brings life to the world.

When you seem to pass by the "things of death"— unmet goals, dissatisfied people, uncooperative team members, or the very real grave of someone who died— know that there is no waste. God has called you personally into His service and has adorned you with gifts that will turn times of tragedy or dissatisfaction into times of blessing. God did it on Easter; He'll do it today.

PRAYER

Heavenly Father, thank You for calling us into ministry. Continually remind us of the uniqueness of this calling. Give us the faith and patience to persevere during trying days until we once again see You turn evil into good. In Jesus' name. Amen.

16

OUR OWN EXODUS

Before God called Moses as their leader, the children of Israel didn't stand out as much of a nation. There may have been a lot of them, but the Israelites had little to unify them, other than slavery and misery. The Passover had not occurred. There wasn't a temple or a king. As Genesis clearly says, the Israelites didn't even know the name of their God. They may have descended from Abraham, but they weren't much of a family. They lacked a "glue" that would bind them together.

The Israelites weren't without glue for long. Together, they saw Egypt, the land of their oppression, saddled by plagues. Together, they slaughtered unblemished lambs and painted their doorposts with the blood of the lambs. Protected from the Angel of Death, together they girded their loins, gulped down a meal, packed their unleavened bread on their backs, and followed Moses into the wilderness. Together, they came to an abrupt halt, stymied by the Red Sea as they watched and probably smelled the dust of Pharaoh's approaching army. Together, they screamed at Moses for getting them into this mess. Together, they held their breath as Moses' outstretched arm split the sea before their eyes. Together, they crossed and then witnessed God's final vengeance on Pharaoh. Together, they watched Sinai transformed. Years of unfaithfulness, apostasy, exile, dispersion, and genocide would follow, but Israel became one people who shared divinely blessed experiences together.

A church staff is a lot like the people of Israel. It may be large or small in number. It may share a common parent, such as denominational affiliation, alma mater, home state, or even the love of God and His people. But that doesn't create a family atmosphere for the staff. Only common experiences create ties that bind the staff into a "family."

When I arrived as senior pastor at my present congregation, I followed a man who had served there for 15 years. Under his guidance, the congregation had started a Christian day school. The faculty and staff of the church and school had been there for more than 10 years.

Shortly after buying a house, enrolling my kids in school, and moving into my office, I realized that the church and school staff had more confidence in their former pastor than they had in me. This made leadership a challenge. I shared my concern about their lack of confidence with the chairman of the school board. "I'm not sure these people are willing to give me a chance," I said. "What do you expect? You're the new kid on the block," he responded.

That wasn't exactly the response I had hoped to hear. It doesn't matter how long I've been here, by yingle (my grandmother is Swedish), I'm the senior pastor, I thought. They have to let me lead. Now, I'm not an unreasonable person. I haven't done anything to hurt any staff member. My last church staff followed me without question (at least that's how I remembered it). I thought about making a big fuss. I also thought about suffering in silence. While I was busy wondering how to become an integral part of this staff, God intervened. He turned a problem into an Exodus experience.

The problem occurred on a Wednesday morning during Advent. I was leading the morning chapel service for our school. To help the children understand Advent, I planned to welcome them to chapel, tell them this was the first Wednesday in Advent, and explain that during Advent we remember that we are waiting for Jesus to return and take us to heaven. Then I was going to make an excuse about forgetting something and hide in the sacristy for a few minutes. When I returned to the chapel, I was going to ask the kids how they felt about the wait. Did they wonder what happened to me? Did they think I had forgotten about them? Did they think maybe I had lied to them about my return? I thought it would prove to be a useful discussion starter.

Because I didn't want to upset the teachers, I talked to them before chapel started. "No matter what I do in chapel this morning, no matter how strange it seems, don't worry and don't move," I said.

Well, I greeted the kids according to plan, made my introductory statements, and started to move quickly toward my exit. I made a Magic Johnson move in what turned out to be a Mother Theresa body. The result wasn't pretty. Specifically, my right foot caught under one of our chancel's open steps, and I fell on top of myself, breaking my right hip in three places.

I learned several things from that experience, one of which was that the staff knew how to follow directions. No one moved a muscle to help me. They sat still in their pews, watching me struggle to stand while they thought to themselves, Isn't he an incredible actor? That fall was so authentic. It seemed like an eternity before someone realized I wasn't acting. The ambulance siren interrupted the silence of the shocked children. They could clearly hear the groans of their pastor as I was wheeled off to the hospital for surgery.

My body may have been broken, but a staff that shared a common past was coming together in a new present for a common mission. We gathered around a shared experience. Together, we saw God deliver His people again. While no sea was parted, hearts were opened wide for a guy who was carried out of the chancel on a stretcher. Every staff member lifted me up in prayer. My accident bound us together as one because it gave us a common story. Everyone played their own role. Some staff members sat quietly thinking nothing was wrong. They tell their story, and we laugh. When some teachers tried to help me, they were fussed at by others who didn't want the illustration spoiled. They tell their story, and we laugh. More than two years after the accident, people still talk about where they were when pastor fell. They share stories about what they thought and felt. When we tell our stories, we still laugh. Sometimes we laugh and hug. That's what families do. Thanks to God's powerful hand, a problem became a blessing. We've been working together every since.

I believe Exodus experiences need to happen again and again among members of a church staff. No, people don't have to experience bodily harm for unity to be achieved. Instead, people become one when they share an experience of God's deliverance of His people.

I've been to hundreds of staff meetings. We have thanked God often for delivering a member or staff person from some trouble. I've been to hundreds of church meetings. We have thanked God for helping our congregation meet its budget or embark on a building program. But what greater deliverance can we celebrate than the family that was baptized because of the loving work of our kindergarten teacher?

Sharing experiences of God's deliverance is so powerful, a staff needs to plan for them. Why not give blood together as a staff? Why not clean up a vacant lot together as a staff? Why not paint a staff member's home together? There are many things that can help bind your staff together, but whatever you do, break a leg and watch God bless.

PRAYER

Father, thank You for entrusting this ministry into our care. Make us a family, Lord. Give us experiences that enable us to bear one another's burdens and so grow in unity to Your glory and to the benefit of Your kingdom. In Jesus' name. Amen.

17

THE CHURCH OF JESUS CHRIST

After years of paying close attention to people as they talk with me about their problems, I've made an observation. When people first discuss their situations, they overuse the pronoun *I*. They can't seem to get their minds off of themselves. *I can't. I won't. I'm afraid. I feel. … I didn't like. … I don't get help …* and on and on it goes. After studying God's Word, praying, and receiving the Lord's Supper, things usually begin to change for the better. As they do, the word *I* almost goes away.

Focusing on oneself makes it almost impossible to serve others. Jesus knew that and enjoined us to "deny [ourselves] and take up [our] cross daily and follow [Him]." It seems that the saints and sinners that make up this body of Christ use the word *I* more often than the word *Jesus*.

If you find yourself in a group of pastors, see how long it takes before one pastor begins talking about *my* church, *my* elders, *my* people, *my* secretary. (You will notice a change only when the discussion turns to the *congregation's* financial troubles.) The point is obvious. Until the pastor takes the congregation's sins on himself, dies for those sins, and rises again for the forgiveness and justification of the members, the congregation doesn't belong to him. It belongs to Jesus. We have been graciously called to serve in *His* church. We minister to *His* people. We are supported by *His* elders and *His* secretary. With that in mind, we are more apt to do *His* will rather than ours.

One day Martin Luther entered the pulpit of the Wittenberg church to feed the flock entrusted to his care. He stood in front of the people, opened his Bible, looked squarely at the congregation, and said, "There is no word of God for you today. Amen." Luther was upset with the people of Wittenberg. He determined that it would be God-pleasing to share only God's Law with the people that day. We have to make the same determination every day as we serve God's people in our congregations. Every church worker occasionally gets frustrated and upset with those they serve. Perhaps a time will come when we need to speak harsh words just as Luther did. But the real question is *whose* word is being spoken to the people of God? Is it *my* word of judgment or is it *God's* Word of judgment?

Preachers, teachers, deaconesses, DCEs, and other church workers can easily find avenues to express their dissatisfaction with those who don't cooperate as they wish. A pastor can easily use the member who disagrees with the use of different worship forms as a sermon illustration of self-centered pride. A teacher seeking an illustration for the Seventh Commandment could easily point out the group of girls who always get to class five minutes late. The DCE who is privy to the sexual experiences of one young person can call people who behave in such ways immoral pagans. Those judgments and statements might make us feel superior, but they do little to maintain or grow the church of Jesus Christ.

Church workers who know that these are not *my* people, *my* students, or *my* youth understand the wisdom of the Scriptures when they direct that if any one sins among us, we, who are spiritual, should correct them with a spirit of gentleness. That's how our Lord deals with problems in *His* church. Gentleness is the only thing that brings positive results.

A pastor friend tells an important story about gentleness. A young woman entered his study and declared that she wanted to be married. As the story unfolded, the pastor discovered that she was the granddaughter of a woman who had been a longtime member but was now in heaven. The young woman's parents had recently become members of the church, but she was a member of a Baptist church. The pastor said he would consider performing her marriage service, but he would want to counsel her and her fiance before agreeing to anything.

The young woman became defensive. "We've already done that with our Baptist pastor in another state," she responded. She added she had a friend in the area who was a Baptist minister. She really wanted him to marry her, but he didn't have a church. It turned out she was really shopping for a church *building*. The pastor took a deep breath and explained that her request was very unusual. He explained that a Baptist wedding in a Lutheran church would be very confusing and perhaps offensive to the congregation he served. "But let's not discount anything yet," the pastor added. "We're here to serve you and your family. Perhaps something can be worked out. Why don't we set up a meeting between you, your fiance, your friend, and myself and see what we can figure out?"

My friend didn't compromise any part of his office or his doctrine, but he did keep a door open for ministry. He could have treated the request as simply absurd, implying to the young woman that she was selfish and narrow-minded. But he didn't. He knew it wasn't *his* church and these people weren't just problems off the street. This young woman and her fiance were the beloved children of God. He treated them with love and gentleness.

A few weeks later, the young woman reappeared in his office. "Could you show me the Lutheran wedding service, please?" she asked. They discussed the differences between the Lutheran service and the Baptist service that she was accustomed to. He showed her which areas of the service could be changed and which areas had to remain the same. She was so impressed with his gentle, patient attitude and his desire to help that she and her husband ultimately joined the church. The pastor shared Christ with them in word and deed, and they embraced Christ and His church.

When this pastor shared his experience at his circuit conference, many thought he had gone too far. "We have principles you know" seemed to echo around the room. The nay-sayers were right. We do have principles.

But the most important principle is to be Christ's witness to everyone everywhere.

The other day I was conducting school chapel. Our teachers work diligently to teach the students that the Lord's house is a special place where they can show they love God by behaving appropriately and reverently. The preschool teachers instruct their students to enter the sanctuary with their hands folded and their heads bowed. It's quite a sight to see all these little kids entering the sanctuary in such a pious manner. On this occasion, there was a problem. One of our little pietists ran right into the end of a pew and fell down. He skinned his elbows. The teacher and I took him outside to see if he needed medical attention. The teacher held him and asked what happened. Between sniffles, the boy answered, "I was so busy being reverent, I forgot where I was headed."

I think the little guy is destined to be a theologian or at least a student of church behavior. We get so concerned about being reverent and correct that we lose sight of where we're going. We reach out to *God's* people, not *our* people. We serve a church and world that needs to hear *God's* word of love, forgiveness, and new hope, not just words of obedience and conformity. We reach out to sinners who need us not only to condemn their sin but to announce and demonstrate the forgiveness of sins earned through the death and resurrection of *our* Lord.

You and I, just like this preschooler, are headed toward a celebration. That celebration requires that we take our eyes off ourselves and place them on Jesus. When that happens, the fun begins. When our eyes are on Jesus, a church's success isn't based on the number who attend but on preaching the Word, administering the sacraments, and offering praise and petitions. Focusing on Jesus keeps us from being concerned about the color of the rest rooms, the carpeting in the narthex, and whether we use individual cups or a common cup for Communion. If Jesus is proclaimed, celebrated, and demonstrated then all is well, regardless of the size, shape, or color of the room or the people. When our eyes are on Jesus, we focus on the stories of our young people that give account of their growing faith rather than basing the success of our youth ministry on the number of kids who appear.

Certainly Jesus cares whether our congregation's buildings are well kept and attractive. And He's concerned with the number of people we reach. But that's the point—let Jesus be concerned about those issues. He will make sure they are resolved quickly and well.

I believe it's true that when trouble enters people's lives, they need to talk about themselves. I also suspect that their need to talk about, and be concerned about, themselves is a source of their troubles. The same goes for congregations. Congregations that are more concerned about themselves than the proclamation of the Gospel are in trouble. Congregations get into trouble when they use *I* or *we* more than the name *Jesus*.

May God grant us the grace to measure every word that comes from our mouths and may every word be directly related to the name that's above all names—Jesus Christ.

Prayer

Father, bless us and change us so that we speak about You more than we speak about ourselves. In Jesus' name. Amen.

18

REPLACE YOURSELF

Volunteers are taught to train replacements to take over when their time of service is completed. I believe church workers should do the same.

Every Christian denomination is having trouble training church workers fast enough to replace those who are retiring. Many factors contribute to this phenomena, but one major reason is the perceived lack of freedom that a professional church worker experiences by virtue of the call. Another reason might be the salary—often too little to support a family. And now educational costs to prepare for service in the church can be astronomical, which, when combined with a low salary, may cause some to avoid church work because they don't want to be in debt for years.

While these are all valid concerns, I don't believe they are the primary reason people aren't entering church careers. I believe young men and women don't see joy on the faces or in the lives of professional church workers they know.

Some of us seem to complain about how overworked and underpaid we are to anyone who will listen. We criticize laypeople who disagree with our actions or our plan of action, sometimes without discretion. Then the people we serve discuss our behavior with everyone who will listen—even their children. It's probably a testimony to the intelligence, if not the spiritual development, of our young people that they don't choose church work as a profession.

We can easily change that trend. We just need to share the joys of ministry with the people we serve. When we speak of the privilege of welcoming people into God's family through Baptism, we help young people see the grandeur of church work. When we refer to funerals as opportunities to celebrate the person's life and the new life received from God, we enable young souls considering their future careers to see a powerfully positive way to spend their lives. When we refer to members as the apostle Paul often did, as the "beloved of God," we show young hearts that church work is really working with and for your "family."

Statistics tell us that working men and women will change their professions at least twice. Such frequent change may indicate how difficult it is to find meaning and purpose in life. Church work provides the ultimate in meaning and purpose. We make an eternal difference in people's lives.

I have been fortunate that every church I've served has sent sons and daughters into professional church work. I always asked what helped them choose a church career. They mentioned two things—first, God's call and second, the example of some church worker who had touched their lives.

Martin Luther said that people should believe God is calling them into full-time church work until He does something to convince them that He isn't. If Luther is correct, and I believe he is, then our young people get a lot of obstacles thrown in their way so they can't hear God's voice clearly.

Fathers, mothers, girlfriends, boyfriends, they all can serve as obstacles to people considering church work. Let's pray that our names never appear on the obstacle list. Instead, let's pray that our lives motivate people to struggle with the possibility of church service. As members see our devotion to the Lord, our commitment to His people, and the satisfaction that this service brings us, they should be moved to evaluate their service to the Lord.

Remember, though, that serving as a catalyst for a young person's dedication to a life of public service to the Lord can be a dangerous thing. Everyone isn't necessarily filled with joy when someone decides to follow Christ's call to the ministry. One member of the church I presently serve visited New Orleans and decided to worship in my previous congregation. She found the people warm and engaging. Word got around quickly that this woman was from the church I had been called to. A woman from the New Orleans church approached the visitor and said, "Tell Pastor Rogers that it's all his fault my son is a struggling pastor now and not a rich engineer." She wasn't kidding. She wanted "better" for her son. But this woman's son is passionately committed to his ministry. He enjoys it. He's good at it. He's a gift to the church. I pray that his mother will be able to rejoice with him in his happiness.

Parental disappointment about the decision to serve as professional church workers is common in a world that places such significance on material possessions. But we can't let that stop us. Our Lord would have us joyfully share information about our calling with others so that His call can be heard loud and clear.

Goals are necessary. Churches regularly set membership and attendance goals. Sunday school administrators establish attendance goals. Churches set financial goals. Schools set goals for enrollment or academic achievement. These are all wonderful. But I believe we need to add one more goal. May each of us make it our goal during our term of ministry to so excite another person that he or she can clearly hear God's call to serve in His church and answer it faithfully. It's the least we can do for a Lord who has so wonderfully provided us with meaning and purpose in life.

PRAYER

Father in heaven, You don't want anyone to stand idle in the marketplace while there's work to do for You. Bless us in our labors so that we may encourage others to dedicate their professional lives to work in Your vineyard. Through Christ our Lord. Amen.

19

PRAYER

I have five books that deal with prayer. I just counted. They speak about the simplicity of prayer, the power of prayer, the need for prayer, the wisdom of prayer, and the blessings of prayer. They are intended to make me a better pray-er.

Teaching someone to pray is an awesome task, after all, prayer is an intimate conversation with the divine. Teaching someone to pray isn't a task we should enter into lightly. Only two people in the Bible really presumed to teach others to pray. One was John the Baptist. The other was our Lord Jesus. The Scriptures don't provide any insight into how John taught his disciples to pray. But the Bible does show us what Jesus taught His disciples.

When the Twelve came to Jesus and asked Him to teach them to pray, He didn't give them a lesson on prayer. He didn't teach them 12 steps to a wonderful prayer life. Instead, He gave them this prayer: "Our Father in heaven, hallowed be Your name, Your kingdom come, Your will be done on earth as it is in heaven. Give us today our daily bread. Forgive us our debts as we also have forgiven our debtors. And lead us not into temptation, but deliver us from the evil one" (Matthew 6:9–13). What Jesus really did was to say, "Let's not talk about praying, let's pray."

That's good news for church workers. You and I don't need one more thing we have to get right. It's nice to know that there's one thing in our lives that we can't goof up. We don't have to think about how to pray, we just need to pray. Let me share an example or two about the difference prayer has made in my life and in the lives of others.

The elders in our church take their prayer responsibilities seriously. We decided to take the words of James as a directive for our ministry: "Is any one of you sick? He should call the elders of the church to pray over him and anoint him with oil in the name of the Lord. And the prayer offered in faith will make the sick person well" (James 5:14–15). The church I serve, and the elders who have been appointed, aren't "charismatic." One elder has said we don't get that excited about anything. When we started to pray for and with sick people, we weren't looking for miracles. We were just following God's instructions. We prayed for people and some of them got well. Some received eternal healing in heaven. We didn't get upset one way or the other; we trusted God was doing what was best.

When a few people died after we had prayed with them, I asked myself why we did this. The answer came from one of the elders. "Pastor, I always feel guilty after we go and pray with someone," he said. I asked why.

"Because I'm convinced this heals me more than it does the person we're praying for," he responded. I think our elder spoke volumes about the power of prayer for all God's people, especially church workers. The one who prays is as blessed as the one who is prayed for.

The enemy attacks us daily. His relentless onslaughts target our weaknesses. Sometimes it seems like we stand alone to face him. We don't always readily express our fears. We lack immediate releases for our anger. Even our joy, if expressed to boisterously, can be misconstrued. God understands all our emotions, and He is ready to hear us.

Church workers have been trained to pray. When we pray in public, people expect us to be as articulate as a best-selling author and as sensitive as a poet. That's a lot of pressure that doesn't come from on high. The earliest prayer offered to our Father was the simple words, "Lord, have mercy." While not long, it's perfectly to the point.

That's all our Lord expects—that we would be perfectly to the point, perfectly frank, perfectly honest, perfectly sincere. One of God's greatest leaders, Moses, enjoyed a frank, sincere prayer life with God. After God scolded him for the behavior of the Israelites, Moses became incensed and told the Lord he was fed up with being responsible for them. He brashly told the Lord that if being the leader of these hard-headed people was all he had to look forward to, he wanted the Lord to kill him. (Frankly, I've felt the same after a few voters' meetings.) God didn't strike Moses dead for his insolence. He loved him, forgave him, and empowered him. God seems to have approved of Moses' openness. God approves of frankness in our prayer lives as well. We are never alone. We have a Father in heaven who will listen to our grief, our pain, and our anger, even when it's directed at Him.

Some would have us think that prayer is a complicated matter. Nothing breaks my heart more than to hear God's children say He didn't answer them because they didn't offer their prayer correctly or with the right attitude. It just doesn't work that way. God loves us way too much to be so arbitrary.

If my 6-year-old daughter says, "Dad, I'm thirsty," I know what she wants. I pour her a glass of milk. If she says, "My dear father, who hath wonderfully provided for all my needs these past six years, thou who hast fed me with every good thing and provided raiment for my body, wouldst thou consider traversing to the rectangular appliance filled with freon and retrieving the plastic canister filled with the fruit of the cow so that I might enjoy it as a libation?" I would still pour her a glass of milk. In fact, if my daughter says, "Moo," I pour her some milk. I know what my child requires. She doesn't need to ask for it in perfect English. It's the same with our heavenly Father. Our words don't need to be perfectly anything. We just need to speak, and He will hear.

Our Father hears our prayers for our congregation. He hears our prayers for those who are ill. He hears our prayers for those who are angry or upset with us. He hears our prayers and He answers. But perhaps the greatest blessing that God gives us when we pray is His peace.

There was a time when doctors thought I was suffering from heart disease. The night before my angiogram, I looked at the cross that I received as a confirmation gift. Most of the night I looked at the cross and prayed through tears. My prayer was only one word—help. God did. His help was more wonderful than I could have imagined. But the strongest answer God gave me was the tremendous peace that came over me that night. I knew the promise God gave me in His Word—no matter what happened in the morning, He would be there to make it good. Prayer brings peace as we remember God's promises.

PRAYER

Lord, teach me to pray. Let my moments with You be filled with honesty and praise. Keep me confident in Your grace so that I will call on You in days of trouble and gladness. In Jesus' name. Amen.

20

SPIRITUAL GROWTH

As a child, I experienced one spiritual crisis after another. My best friend in sixth grade was the son of a Baptist preacher. This man must have discussed the book of Revelation with his son often. My friend would come to school on Monday mornings and tell me how the moon was going to turn to blood and the earth was going to be consumed with fire on the last day. He also told me about this thing called the rapture where Christians are graciously lifted (or jerked) out of this world so that they miss all the moon-turning-to-blood stuff that everybody else has to deal with.

This rapture stuff provided little comfort for a Lutheran boy who spent a lot of time on California freeways. The thought of God suddenly leaving thousands of cars without drivers didn't seem like the best solution to me, but what did I know—I was just a Lutheran. In my mind, the only suitable explanation for the rapture was that the people who drove the freeways every day weren't Christians. That made sense to me because I had watched freeway drivers for years. No one's behavior looked very sanctified to me. My friend also told me that these end-of-the-world changes would be announced by Gabriel, who would sound a trumpet.

The house I grew up in is seven miles from Los Angeles International Airport. Just imagine a Boeing 737 taking off over your house. It can sound pretty similar to Gabriel's trumpet to a boy whose best friend has a book-of-Revelation preaching dad. I was convinced we were going to heaven about 10 times a day. In those days, I had no trouble fearing God.

My parents and Sunday school teachers always told me I would have all my God questions answered when I hit confirmation class. I went faithfully for two years, trudging two miles up hill through the snow both ways (even Southern Californians tell that story to their confirmation-age kids who complain about attending class). But I didn't get my questions answered. In fact, I had more questions. The biggest question I had regarded the ability to "discern the body of the Lord" (1 Corinthians 11:29, my translation). My pastor explained that a worthy communicant must be able to discern the truth that Jesus is truly in, with, and under the bread and wine. *Discern*, he explained, meant to understand and to know for sure that Jesus was there.

I tried very hard to "discern the body of the Lord" but for the life of me, I couldn't. How on earth could Jesus inhabit the everyday bread and wine and not make it look different? I really believed that God could do it on His own, but I couldn't understand it so I could tell someone else. Therefore, I was sure I didn't "know" enough to take Communion.

The day of my confirmation drew near. I could give all the right answers, I just couldn't understand all the answers I gave. A week after the rite of confirmation came the reception of my first Communion. That's how we did things in our church made up of Midwesterners who had settled in California. (I've always taken offense when people tell me that Californians are crazy, as if this state caused their insanity. I can discern this truth—crazy Californians are really Midwesterners with arthritis.) I was only too happy to be confirmed. It meant I got my Saturday mornings back. But to take Communion—that was too much. I knew that if I took it unworthily—and I knew I was unworthy because I didn't understand—I would be eating and drinking judgment on myself. As far as I was concerned, I was going to hell if I took Communion.

I told my parents that I would be confirmed but that I would pass on first Communion. My mother got more upset then my pastor did when we didn't know our memory work. She told me that my grandparents, my aunts and uncles, and my cousins were coming from all over to be there for my first Communion and I had to go. The options were clear. I could take Communion and go to hell, or I could stay away from Communion and make my mother angry. The decision was clear too. It would be far easier to go to hell than to suffer the consequences of my angry mother. I would take Communion.

These stories show a young man in spiritual crisis, a young man who, by the grace and power of God, has changed. We have all experienced spiritual growth. Many well-intentioned people have provided me with pamphlets from church's that make claims that attending a seminar or conference will enable you to grow spiritually. I've gone, but what I've heard is talk about how God will prove Himself strong to those who *allow* Him to do so. I've heard talk about how God can make us grow when *we give* Him "quiet time" in which to work. I've listened to lectures that tell me that God will make me grow once *I give* Him control of my life. With all due respect, the only thing that really grew was the thought that I and only I could bring about my spiritual growth. If that were the case, I would still be running from jumbo jets and refusing to take Communion. If I didn't create my spirituality, if that were a gift from on high, then how can I believe that I can contribute to the growth of this thing that I didn't make?

Where does spiritual growth come from if it doesn't come from churches that publish four-color brochures? It comes from powerfully simple places and things. It comes from the Word as it is read and the sacraments as they are administered. It comes through the fellowship of Christian people who gather around Word and Sacrament and celebrate the fact that the God who raised Jesus from the dead will also see them through trouble and tragedy.

Louise was in her late 60s when I met her in New Orleans. She had been blessed with one child. Clifford was born with severe mental problems. He was in his 30s when I met him. Louise made sure he attended church each Sunday. They lived within walking distance of the church so they wouldn't have to miss. Louise's husband had died very young, many years before I arrived on the scene.

I always believed that Louise had as many challenges as anyone could have, but I was wrong. One day Louise sent word that she had been diagnosed with a brain tumor. If that weren't enough to think about, what would happen to Clifford? He had never been separated from his mother and was incapable of understanding what was happening to her. Louise tried to explain the problem to Clifford, and then she entered the hospital for surgery. Clifford went to a cousin's home to wait for his mother's return. He never saw her again.

Louise came through surgery successfully, but the night after her surgery, Clifford died. The center of Louise's life was taken from her as she lay in critical condition following brain surgery. We wondered whether she should be told. Her surgeon told me there was no "good" time to tell someone news like this. It was likely to do her more damage to hear the news weeks later than right away.

I told Louise, her head covered in bandages, that her only son had died. Tears filled her eyes as we tried to comfort her with words and hugs. I remember looking at her tear-stained face as she uttered the words, "Now the Lord has answered all of my prayers." After her husband died, Louise had prayed that the Lord would take her son first so that he would never be alone in this "veil of tears." I was, and am, amazed at her love and faith. Now I know how Jesus felt when He said He had never seen such faith as that of the woman who longed to eat the crumbs that fell from the master's table. As I shared God's Word and the Holy Meal with Louise, her faith helped my faith grow.

One Sunday afternoon, I was listening to a football game. It was no ordinary football game. If the New Orleans Saints won, it would be their first winning season in their 20-year history. The phone interrupted the game. The voice on the other end belonged to a young lady who was a member of our youth group. She said she needed to meet with me. Right now. I met her at church, but she wasn't alone. With her was a young man who had fathered the baby she would have in seven months.

The young couple wanted to keep the baby and asked me to marry them. I agreed to marry them and, through much counseling, promised to be with them no matter what. They were married. They had a beautiful girl, but she had serious heart problems. From the first day of her life, she needed special care and therapy. Doctors hoped to keep her alive until she was 2 years old. At that age, they thought she would be strong enough to survive surgery to repair her heart and allow her to live a normal life.

The day finally arrived for Brittany's surgery. But it didn't go well. Brittany's little body couldn't recover from the insult it sustained in surgery. One incredibly difficult week later, doctors told the parents Brittany had suffered brain death. Doctors urged her parents to take their baby off the respirator that was keeping her alive.

When the difficult decision was finally made, great-grandparents, grandparents, aunts, uncles, and friends crowded into the intensive care unit. Each family member and friend held the tiny child. After dozens of people had held Brittany and told her good-bye, the intricate machinery was disconnected from her body. God welcomed her into eternity.

As the tubes were disconnected, her parents held her. Her mother cried as she held Brittany. She seemed to cry for an eternity. A nurse stood ready to take Brittany away, but her young mother wouldn't give her up. The nurse asked me to do something.

I knelt beside the mother and asked if she remembered the story of Jesus and the little children. I asked if she could see Jesus holding the little children on His lap. She nodded yes. I asked if she could see Brittany on Jesus' lap. She said yes. Then I asked her to give Brittany to me because Brittany was no longer here. She is on Jesus' lap. To my amazement, she handed the child to me. Once this 18-year-old mother was reminded that Jesus held her baby, she was ready to let her body go. The faith she exhibited during that trial enabled my faith to grow.

We church workers encounter many plans and programs carrying a "faith-growing" guarantee. As long as they are centered in Word and Sacrament, God's Holy Spirit will use them to help us grow spiritually. We also can share with one another the faith experiences of the people we serve. What the Spirit does in others, He can also do in us.

Let it be our prayer that God would enable us to put our feet in the same places as the people we serve. And may God so grace and bless us that our faith may one day be the Spirit's tool for increasing someone's faith.

PRAYER

Lord Jesus, You strengthen Your people so that they bear mighty witness to You. This witness strengthens the faith of all who are privileged to see it. May we grow through the witness of the people we serve, and may our faith be so plain that we serve as a source of strength for others. We ask it in Your name. Amen.

21

THIS CHURCH NEEDS A FEW TEAM PLAYERS

"If opinions could fly, this place would be an airport," one person commented after a staff meeting. She was correct. We have a number of strong-willed people on our staff, and sometimes our strong wills prove to be problematic. We've counted the number of oldest children on the staff, thinking that might be the problem. It turns out that oldest children are actually in the minority. We've counted the number of Germans on the staff. (Those of us non-Germans were absolutely sure that was the problem.) But we actually have more Scandinavians than Germans. Someone even asked how many of us were born under the astrological sign of Taurus, the hard-headed bull. We decided that consulting the horoscope really wasn't appropriate, much less Christian. We were stumped. How did we get so opinionated?

We all hit on the answer simultaneously. The source of the stubborn streak lies with the college or seminary we attended. To be completely honest, the colleges and seminaries aren't completely at fault, but they do bear some responsibility. Nowhere in our training were we required to take a course called Teamwork 101. Instead, most of us were trained to work as independent practitioners. We learned that we bore sole responsibility for all things around the church. Nothing could be further from the truth. Any ministry, whether with 25 professionals or just one, is a team because we all work for and with the team leader, Jesus Christ. Church workers need to become consummate team players. Thankfully, we all take our place under the leadership and lordship of Christ. He leads, guides, directs, admonishes, and praises us.

I've closely observed several church ministry teams that work and several that don't work. It helped me isolate factors that make team ministry work. I received input from team members themselves as they answered two questions. First, is your team ministry happy and healthy? Second, what makes it happy or unhappy? I found no middle ground as I evaluated team ministries. They either worked great or they didn't seem to work at all. When they function well, they are very good. When they function poorly, they are horrid.

A number of factors contribute to good team ministry: humility, a love for the Lord, the ability to handle criticism, a safe psychological environment, and people who know how to have fun, to name a few. The factors that point to a poor team ministry include team members who are megalomaniacs, defensive attitudes, people who believe they're the only ones with the right answers, lack of concern for ministry, and a lack of "vision" for the church. While these all contribute to the failure of team ministry, I think it all boils down to one issue—friendship. The most successful ministry teams are those where the individuals count Christ as their best friend and have befriended one another.

Countless hours and dollars have been spent helping church workers learn to plan together, vision together, communicate with one another, and resolve conflicts with one another. Maybe it would have been better to use our time and financial resources to give church workers money and free time to go out with one another and learn to be friends. I speak from experience.

My first position was as an associate pastor in a church where the senior pastor had been there 20 years. In our first few meetings, he indicated that he wasn't sure he wanted a coworker but the congregation thought it was a good idea. It was less than a warm welcome. Both of us were new to "team ministry," but by the grace of God, and the grace of God alone, we took our first step in team ministry. And it was the right one.

We didn't call a consultant. We didn't call the circuit counselor or the district president. We went to a football game. We found one thing in common. We told stories about football games we had seen. We discussed our favorite players. After the game, we each ate a dozen oysters and a dozen boiled Louisiana blue crabs. Before we knew it, we had moved past football and on to our families, our successes, and our failures. We even talked about our hope for the church. It struck us both—we were having fun.

We became friends first, colleagues second. That friendship, and its foundation of appreciation and respect, enabled us to communicate honestly, to encourage each other in our assignments, to rejoice when the other did well, and to be the first one there when the other was down. I stood by him the Sunday we feared he had had a heart attack while preaching. He was there when I had ankle surgery. He helped me out when my house was robbed. I consoled him when his mother died. The congregation saw us as a team. Our supporters loved it; our detractors despised it. They realized they couldn't divide this union.

Because I was on a team with a friend, ministry was fun. We laughed often with each other and with the congregation. When a venerable charter member died, the family asked us to travel about 100 miles to her hometown to jointly celebrate the funeral. We happily agreed. On the way to this little Mississippi town, we had car trouble, locked the keys in the trunk, and got lost. When we arrived at the funeral home (thankfully on time), we were both exhausted.

One of the woman's lifelong friends sang a solo at the beginning of the service. The woman's voice probably sounded great in the shower, but out in public, it left something to be desired. Besides being a little flat in pitch, the woman was a little heavy. (I'm trying to put the best construction on everything.) In my tired, frustrated, exhausted state, I couldn't help but make a comment. "Let's go," I whispered to my teammate and friend. "The service is over." He looked at me quizzically and asked what I meant. "The fat lady just sang!" I answered.

I should have remembered that the funeral director had clipped a microphone to my colleague's stole, but I didn't. The congregation heard my comment loud and clear. Some laughed. Some didn't. I haven't been asked to do a funeral in that town since. But the experience galvanized a wonderful relationship. I was out of line. I knew it, and my friend knew it. He never used my indiscretion against me. Instead, he forgave me, laughed with me, and continues to remind others of it when he gets the chance.

Teams are powerful. When everyday, run-of-the-mill people work together as a team, I believe they can become great. New Orleans has many famous events besides Mardi Gras. One such event is a 10K run called the Crescent City Classic. For years the race took place on Palm Sunday. Many of our elders, ushers, Sunday school teachers, and choir members ran. Each year, they had to decide whether to be faithful to the Lord or to run in this race. It broke our hearts to see faithful members placed in such a quandary, and frankly, it fried our toes to think that the planners could be so insensitive to hold the race on a Sunday.

The senior pastor and I wrote a satirical letter to the editor of the city paper. We told the event planners that "preachers were pounding their pulpits in a panic on the Sunday of Palms because they wanted to be pounding their toes on the turf of the race." We stated that "terribly scarce tenors" were absent, causing choir directors to become "terribly ticked." We could no longer assure event planners that we could control the choir directors who were demanding revenge. The event planners needed to make some changes. The editorial ran on Easter Sunday. Neither of us saw it, so it took us by surprise when worshipers greeted us with "You guys got published!" instead of the traditional, powerful Easter greeting, "He is risen!" The next year, the race took place on Saturday. We accomplished more together than we could ever do alone.

The team I serve with today also appreciates one another and enjoys having a good time. Sometimes the pastors are lovingly chastised by the worshipers because of the laughing and smiling we do in our seats. They may tease us about having a good time, but I think they appreciate that we get along. Members have heard too many stories about professional ministry teams that have crashed on the rocks of pride and arrogance. It does their hearts good to see their leaders getting along. Church workers who cooperate foster a mood and expectation among members that encourages them to get along with one another.

The members here know that their professional church workers disagree and argue occasionally. They also know we resolve differences without incident and continue to serve the Lord together. Because of this attitude, the members do the same. Nothing makes me feel better than to see two members who have been at odds during a congregation meeting put their arms around each other and laugh at the conclusion of the meeting. Others can easily see their friendship.

The people we work with are precious. They come from the very hand of God as His gifts to the church. Our parents would be proud to hear us call these people friends. So let's work on those friendships. To make friendship possible at the church I presently serve, I keep asking the congregation to budget for things like season tickets to sports events, concerts, and plays. I would use these tickets to help church workers build friendships. I haven't been successful yet, but I hope to be.

You can help. Ask your congregation to place money for entertainment tickets in your budget. If you get it first, then I'm sure that will set a precedent, and other churches will fall in line like dominoes. That's what I call teamwork.

PRAYER

Father, in Christ Jesus You changed us from being Your enemies to being Your friends. May that friendship permeate our team ministry which You lead. Grant it for Jesus' sake. Amen.

22

Personal and Professional Growth—Don't Let This Happen to You

I happened to sit in first class on a plane trip from New Orleans to Houston. On this particular trip, I was privileged to sit next to an astronaut. He was a gregarious fellow who wanted to talk about what he did for a living and sort of hear what I did for a living.

For the first 40 minutes of the one-hour trip, I listened to the astronaut hold forth on weightlessness, space stations, new technologies, and black holes. When he finished, he asked me what I did for a living. I told him I was a minister. His ho-hum look motivated me to describe my work in as exciting a manner as possible. I told him about everything from Dead Sea scrolls to breakthroughs in counseling techniques.

I did my best, but the man still looked bored. So I asked what he thought about my profession. "Well, I guess it's okay, but it doesn't sound very exciting," he said. "In fact, it sounds like that same old story, 'Jesus loves me this I know, for the Bible tells me so.' "

The man perceived church work as a profession that didn't provide any opportunity for professional growth. I wasn't pleased. In fact, I was incensed at his pride. "It seems to me that you have the same problem with sameness," I told him. He was stunned and asked what I meant. "Didn't you listen when I told you about all our advancements?" he asked. I replied that I had but that it all sounded like the same "twinkle, twinkle, little star. How I wonder what you are" to me. That's when we landed in Houston. He left the plane in silence—quickly.

That encounter exhibited mutual pride. He was proud of the contribution he and his discipline were making to the world. I was taking seriously the good we do in church work. But that conversation made me think. The astronaut made sure he was up-to-date on current discoveries affecting his work. I couldn't say the same. Although things are improving, church workers still need to be responsible for professional growth. It's an issue of professional pride. What emphasis do we put on our profession and the services we perform for God and His people? Do we prize it enough to deliberately schedule time for improvement of our skills? Or will we happily function at a 1960 performance level in the new century?

It's easy to argue that advances in our professions haven't kept pace with other disciplines. After all, the

Bible hasn't changed in almost 2,000 years. We still baptize people. We still celebrate Communion just as our Lord instituted it and as Paul instructed the church at Corinth to almost 20 centuries ago. Our message hasn't changed. But isn't it good to know that some things don't change?

The Gospel we preach does not change, but the people we speak it to change continuously. Some church workers remember when marriages survived at a much higher rate than today's 50 percent. Parents used to be more free to help out at school and church. Confirmation schedules of yesteryear didn't have to be built around parental visitation rights. Worship leaders seemed to more easily agree what music styles were effective for congregations. But that has all changed. Those who communicate the Gospel of Jesus Christ need to know and learn about these and similar changes or we will miss many opportunities to bring the Good News to new generations.

At the turn of the century, one of America's most successful companies was a leather works. It made seats and whips for horse-drawn carriages. Within a few years, they went out of business. Had someone mishandled the finances? No, someone mishandled change. Henry Ford had invented the horseless carriage—the automobile. Whips weren't needed anymore. But didn't the automobile need seats? Why couldn't this company have provided Ford with padded benches for his horseless carriage? Maybe it could have if it had kept up with the changing world.

We don't want this story to be repeated in the church. Education is the key. Church workers should take continuing education as seriously as other professionals do. After all, the fruits of our professional growth aren't temporal, they're eternal. Teachers in the public sector think nothing of attending school every summer to maintain their credentials. May the day come when pastors, DCEs, deaconesses, day school teachers, and others spend time each year honing their skills and broadening their knowledge for the Lord.

But what about the potential obstacles to professional growth? In 1984, I asked the congregation I served for permission to enter a graduate studies program. I explained that after five years in the field, my "well was running dry." I needed to fill it up. They gave permission. I applied, was accepted, and began to plan to attend classes. Then my wife mentioned we were expecting another child. I decided that my family responsibilities took precedence, so I deferred my plans for continuing my education. In 1986, I decided to try again. Again the congregation supported my endeavor, with one concern. We were beginning a capital fund drive to build a much-needed education building. Again, I decided it would be best to postpone my studies. Two years later another building program prevented me from enrolling. Two years later I took a call to California. I felt it would be inappropriate to ask a new congregation for permission to resume my studies. To make this long story short, I've been out of the seminary for 15 years and I still haven't done anything about continuing education. While my reasons for postponing it were all appropriate, I'm having second-thoughts. God's people deserve church workers that maintain their skills. That's well worth the investment of time and money.

Involving yourself in professional growth activities blesses many people. It blesses the people you serve as they experience your improved skills, but it also blesses your present and future coworkers. Present coworkers may be inspired, even forced, to continue their own education. And future coworkers may find it easier to get permission to further their education because the congregation sees the blessings such continuing education brings.

You and I certainly can't do anything to change the minds of those who believe the church is outmoded and outdated. But we don't have to add grist to the mill by neglecting our responsibility to grow as church professionals. Unlike "Twinkle, twinkle, little star," Jesus loves me is more than a nursery rhyme. It is a call to life, a call to service, and a call to growth—professional growth.

PRAYER

Father, help us grow in knowledge and skill as we serve Your people. Grant that we are never satisfied with our skills but always seek to improve them in response to Your love for us. In Jesus' name. Amen.